Breakthrough to Brilliance

Unleashing Your Creative Genius:

Unlock Your Creative Potential and Innovate Your Life

BY
ADEEL ANJUM

CONTENTS

INTRODUCTION 1

Part 1: Igniting the Creative Flame

Chapter 01
Embracing Curiosity 5
Chapter 02
Defeating the Inner Critic 10
Chapter 03
Rekindling Your Inner Child 15
Chapter 04
The Power of Constraints 22
Chapter 05
Embracing the Messy Middle 29
Chapter 06
The Inspiration Playground 35
Chapter 07
Rethinking Your Routine 41
Chapter 08
The Power of Collaboration 47

Part 2: Cultivating Your Creative Arsenal

Chapter 09
The Magic of Mind Maps 53
Chapter 10
The Art of Reframing 59
Chapter 11
Design Thinking for Innovation 64

Chapter 12
The Power of "Yes, And..." Improvisation 71
Chapter 13
Embracing Randomness and Serendipity 78
Chapter 14
Hacking Your Creativity 84
Chapter 15
Building a Creative Habit 89
Chapter 16
Sharpening Your Creative Saw 95

Part 3: Igniting Innovation in Your Life

Chapter 17
Innovation at Work 102
Chapter 18
Reimagining Your Daily Routine 111
Chapter 19
Design Thinking for Personal Challenges 117
Chapter 20
Innovation in Relationships 123
Chapter 21
The Art of Creative Problem-Solving 130
Chapter 22
Innovation on a Budget 136
Chapter 23
The Innovation Mindset for Lifelong Learning 142
Chapter 24
Leaving Your Creative Legacy 147
Chapter 25
The Innovation Journey Never Ends 152

CONCLUSION   **157**

INTRODUCTION

In a world brimming with possibilities, there exists an unseen spark—an extraordinary potential residing within each and every one of us, waiting to be ignited. This spark, this essence of creativity and innovation, holds the key to unlocking a life of limitless possibilities and boundless fulfillment. Welcome to the journey of self-discovery, where we embark on a quest to uncover the depths of our unique brilliance and unleash the extraordinary within.

Beyond Limits

Too often, we find ourselves constrained by the limitations imposed upon us—by society, by circumstance, and most of all, by our own beliefs. We are told to conform, to follow the well-trodden path, and to suppress the whispers of our innermost desires. But what if we dared to defy these limits? What if we challenged the status quo and dared to dream beyond the boundaries of what's deemed possible? It's time to shatter the shackles of limiting beliefs and societal expectations that confine us and embrace the vast expanse of our potential.

A Guide to Self-Discovery

This book serves as a compass—a guiding light on your journey of self-discovery and personal transformation. Within these pages, you'll find a roadmap for unlocking your unique brilliance, navigating the twists and turns of your inner landscape, and uncovering the hidden treasures that lie dormant within you. Each chapter is a stepping stone—a doorway leading you deeper into the heart of who you are and who you have the power to become.

Unlocking Happiness and Fulfillment

At the heart of this journey lies a profound truth: self-discovery is the key to unlocking happiness and fulfillment in life. By peeling back the layers of conditioning, expectation, and conformity, we reveal the essence of our true selves—the source of our deepest joys and most profound satisfactions. As we embrace our authenticity and lean into our passions, we tap into a wellspring of creativity, purpose, and meaning that infuses every aspect of our lives.

Throughout this book, we'll explore the profound connection between self-discovery and creating a life of purpose and significance. We'll delve into the depths of our innermost desires, uncovering the dreams that have long lain dormant within us and setting them ablaze with the fire of possibility. Together, we'll embark on a journey of exploration, growth, and transformation—a journey that promises to illuminate the path to a life of extraordinary fulfillment and boundless joy.

So, are you ready to unlock the extraordinary within? Are you prepared to challenge the limits of what's possible and embrace the fullness of your potential? If so, then join me as we embark on this exhilarating adventure of self-discovery and personal transformation. The journey awaits, and the possibilities are endless.

Part 1: Igniting the Creative Flame

Chapter 01

Embracing Curiosity

In a world overflowing with information, it's easy to fall into the trap of assuming we already know enough. But true creativity begins with a simple yet powerful trait: curiosity. When we embrace curiosity, we open ourselves to a world of possibilities, constantly seeking to understand, explore, and innovate.

Cultivating a Curious Mind

Curiosity is the driving force behind discovery and innovation. It's about asking questions, no matter how unconventional they may seem, and being genuinely interested in the answers. Cultivating a curious mind means actively seeking out new experiences, ideas, and perspectives. It's about challenging assumptions and being open to the unknown.

One way to cultivate curiosity is by adopting a growth mindset. Instead of seeing challenges as obstacles, view them as opportunities for learning and growth. Embrace the idea that intelligence and abilities can be developed through dedication and hard work. This mindset encourages a sense of curiosity and a willingness to explore new territory.

To nurture curiosity, make a conscious effort to engage with the world around you. Pay attention to the small details, notice patterns, and ask yourself why things are the way they are. Keep a journal to jot down questions, observations, and ideas that pique your interest. By actively engaging with your surroundings, you'll cultivate a sense of wonder and curiosity that fuels your creativity.

Identifying Your "Ignorance Gaps"

To truly embrace curiosity, it's essential to acknowledge what we don't know. This involves identifying our "ignorance gaps" – areas where our knowledge or understanding is limited. Rather than viewing ignorance as a weakness, see it as an opportunity for growth. By recognizing our gaps in knowledge, we can take proactive steps to fill them.

Start by reflecting on your own areas of expertise and where you feel less confident. What topics or skills do you wish you knew more about? What questions do you find yourself pondering? Take inventory of your ignorance gaps and prioritize areas you'd like to explore further.

Seeking knowledge from diverse sources is key to expanding our understanding. Engage with people who have different perspectives and expertise, read books outside of your comfort zone, and explore topics that challenge your assumptions. Embracing diversity in thought and experience enriches our understanding of the world and fuels our curiosity.

Consider joining discussion groups, attending workshops, or enrolling in courses related to your areas of interest. Embrace opportunities for lifelong learning and approach new challenges with an open mind. By actively seeking out knowledge and expertise, you'll broaden your horizons and deepen your curiosity.

Learning from Children's Natural Curiosity

Children are natural-born explorers, approaching the world with boundless curiosity and wonder. They ask endless questions, eager to understand how things work and why things are the way they are. As adults, we can learn a great deal from this childlike curiosity.

Take inspiration from children by approaching life with a sense of playfulness and wonder. Allow yourself to be fascinated by the world around you, finding joy in simple discoveries. Engage in activities that stimulate your imagination and encourage creative thinking, whether it's doodling in a sketchbook, experimenting with new recipes in the kitchen, or taking long walks in nature.

Children also have a remarkable ability to embrace failure and learn from their mistakes. They're not afraid to try new things or make a mess in the process. As adults, we often become more risk-averse, fearing failure and the judgment of others. But failure is an essential part of the creative process. Embrace the mindset of a beginner, be willing to make mistakes, and learn from each experience along the way.

Sparking Creativity Through Fresh Eyes

Creativity thrives on novelty and fresh perspectives.

One way to spark creativity is by looking at the world with fresh eyes, seeing familiar things from new angles and with a renewed sense of wonder. Challenge yourself to break out of routine and embrace spontaneity.

Traveling to new places, meeting new people, and immersing yourself in different cultures can provide fresh insights and inspire creativity. But you don't have to travel far to see the world differently. Simply changing your daily routine, trying new hobbies, or exploring unfamiliar neighborhoods can shake up your perspective and ignite your creative spark.

Practice mindfulness to cultivate a deeper awareness of the present moment. Slow down and savor the sights, sounds, and sensations around you. Notice the beauty in the ordinary and find inspiration in unexpected places. By embracing mindfulness, you'll cultivate a sense of presence that fuels your creativity and deepens your connection to the world.

In conclusion, embracing curiosity is the first step toward unlocking your creative potential. By cultivating a curious mind, identifying your ignorance gaps, learning from children's natural curiosity, and looking at the world with fresh eyes, you can ignite the creative flame within you and embark on a journey of endless discovery and innovation. So, dare to ask questions, explore the unknown, and embrace the joy of curiosity.

Chapter 02

Defeating the Inner Critic

Creativity often dances hand in hand with vulnerability. Yet, as we strive to unleash our creative genius, there's a formidable foe lurking within us: the inner critic. This voice, fueled by self-doubt and fear of judgment, can sabotage our efforts and stifle our creativity. But fear not, for defeating the inner critic is not only possible but essential for unlocking our full creative potential.

Identifying Negative Self-Talk

The first step in overcoming the inner critic is recognizing its insidious whispers. Negative self-talk takes many forms, from harsh self-criticism to crippling doubt. Phrases like "I'm not good enough,""It's a bad idea," or "I'll never succeed" can echo in our minds, casting doubt on our abilities and suffocating our creative spark.

Take a moment to reflect on your own inner dialogue. What negative beliefs or self-limiting beliefs do you frequently encounter? Recognize that these thoughts are not facts but rather conditioned patterns of thinking that can be challenged and overcome.

Journaling can be a powerful tool for uncovering and confronting negative self-talk. Set aside time each day to write down your thoughts and feelings without judgment. Notice any recurring themes or patterns of negativity. By shining a light on these inner shadows, you can begin to dismantle their power over you.

Developing Strategies to Silence the Inner Critic

Once you've identified the negative self-talk, it's time to take action to silence the inner critic. One powerful strategy is reframing your thoughts. Instead of dwelling on self-doubt and criticism, consciously choose to focus on your strengths and past successes. Replace negative statements with positive affirmations that bolster your confidence and belief in your creative abilities.

For example, if the inner critic whispers, "I'm not good enough," counter it with affirmations such as "I am talented and capable," or "I have the creativity and skills to succeed." By reframing your thoughts in this way, you can gradually rewire your brain to adopt a more positive and empowering mindset.

Practice self-compassion by treating yourself with the same kindness and understanding you would offer to a friend. When you make a mistake or encounter setbacks, instead of berating yourself, offer words of encouragement and support. Remember that nobody is perfect, and failure is an inevitable part of the creative journey.

Another effective technique is to embrace the power of "what if." Instead of succumbing to fear and self-doubt, allow yourself to entertain bold and imaginative possibilities. What if your wildest ideas were not only possible but achievable? By embracing curiosity and openness to experimentation, you can silence the inner critic and unleash your creative potential.

Granting Yourself Permission to Fail

One of the most potent weapons against the inner critic is the permission to fail. Failure is not the opposite of success but rather a stepping stone on the path to mastery. Grant yourself the freedom to take risks, make mistakes, and learn from failure without judgment or self-criticism.

Embrace the mindset of a beginner, approaching each creative endeavor with a sense of curiosity and experimentation. Understand that failure is an essential part of the creative process and an opportunity for growth and learning. Celebrate your efforts, regardless of the outcome, and use each setback as a chance to refine your skills and refine your approach.

Remember that creativity thrives in an environment of openness and vulnerability. By embracing the uncertainty and imperfection inherent in the creative process, you can silence the inner critic and unleash your full creative potential.

Developing resilience is essential for overcoming the fear of failure. Cultivate resilience by focusing on your progress rather than perfection. Set realistic goals and celebrate small victories along the way. When faced with challenges, remind yourself of past successes and your ability to overcome obstacles.

Practice self-care to nourish your body, mind, and

spirit. Make time for activities that bring you joy and replenish your energy, whether it's spending time in nature, practicing mindfulness, or engaging in creative pursuits. By prioritizing your well-being, you'll build the strength and resilience needed to silence the inner critic and thrive as a creative individual.

In conclusion, defeating the inner critic is essential for unlocking your creative genius. By identifying negative self-talk, developing strategies to silence the inner critic, embracing the power of "what if," and granting yourself permission to fail, you can cultivate a mindset of resilience, courage, and creativity. So, silence the inner critic, trust in your abilities, and let your creative brilliance shine.

Chapter 03

Rekindling Your Inner Child

Do you remember the boundless imagination and endless curiosity you possessed as a child? The world was a playground of possibilities, and every moment was an opportunity for adventure and discovery. Yet, as we grow older, we often lose touch with that playful spirit, consumed by the responsibilities and pressures of adulthood. But within each of us lies a dormant spark waiting to be reignited – the spirit of our inner child. In this chapter, we'll explore how to rekindle that inner flame and unleash the creative power of our youthful selves.

Reconnecting with Playful Imagination

One of the keys to rekindling your inner child is reconnecting with your playful imagination. As children, we effortlessly slipped into imaginary worlds, transforming cardboard boxes into castles and backyard adventures into epic quests. But somewhere along the way, we traded our capes for suits and ties, forgetting the joy of make-believe.

Take time to reconnect with the playful spirit that lies dormant within you. Engage in activities that ignite your imagination and inspire creativity. Doodle in a sketchbook, build sandcastles at the beach, or lose yourself in a whimsical novel. Give yourself permission to explore without inhibition, embracing the joy of creativity for its own sake.

Indulge in nostalgia by revisiting childhood activities that brought you joy. Dig out old toys or games from your childhood and allow yourself to experience the same sense of wonder and excitement you felt as a child. Whether it's flying kites, blowing bubbles, or playing with action figures, embrace the opportunity to reconnect with your inner child and unleash your creativity.

Incorporating Elements of Play

Incorporating elements of play into your daily life can help rekindle your inner child and stimulate your creativity. Experiment with open-ended games and activities that encourage spontaneity and exploration. Play with building blocks, solve puzzles, or engage in improvisational storytelling.

Give yourself permission to be silly and embrace the absurd. Dance like nobody's watching, sing at the top of your lungs, or make funny faces in the mirror. Playfulness is a powerful antidote to the seriousness of adulthood, allowing you to let go of inhibitions and embrace the joy of creative expression.

Embracing the Joy of Learning

Children possess an insatiable thirst for knowledge and a natural curiosity about the world around them. As adults, we can learn a great deal from their approach to learning. Embrace the joy of discovery and approach problems with a sense of wonder and curiosity.

Take up a new hobby or pursue a topic that fascinates you, purely for the joy of learning. Whether it's mastering a musical instrument, learning a new language, or exploring the mysteries of the universe, embrace the process of discovery with childlike enthusiasm. Allow yourself to be a beginner again, relishing the journey of exploration and growth.

Create opportunities for experiential learning by immersing yourself in new environments and cultures. Travel to unfamiliar destinations, sample exotic foods, and engage with people from different backgrounds. Embrace the discomfort of stepping outside your comfort zone and allow yourself to be transformed by new experiences.

Finding Humor and Lightheartedness

Humor is a powerful tool for breaking down barriers and fostering creativity. Laughter has a way of opening our minds and freeing us from the constraints of self-doubt and judgment. Embrace the lightheartedness of the creative process and find humor in the absurdity of life.

Don't take yourself too seriously. Embrace your quirks and imperfections, and approach challenges with a sense of humor and playfulness. Surround yourself with people who lift your spirits and share your sense of humor. Laughter is contagious, and a playful attitude can infuse your creative endeavors with joy and spontaneity.

Practicing Mindfulness and Presence

Incorporating mindfulness practices into your daily routine can help you reconnect with your inner child and cultivate a sense of presence and wonder. Take time to savor the simple pleasures of life – the warmth of the sun on your skin, the sound of birdsong in the morning, the taste of your favorite meal.

Engage your senses fully in each moment, allowing yourself to experience the world with childlike wonder and curiosity. Release the burdens of the past and the worries of the future, and immerse yourself fully in the present moment. By cultivating mindfulness and presence, you can rekindle your inner child and unlock the creative potential that lies within you.

Creating a Playful Environment

Design your living or workspace to reflect your playful spirit and inspire creativity. Surround yourself with colors, textures, and objects that spark joy and ignite your imagination. Incorporate elements of whimsy and fun into your environment, whether it's decorating with vibrant artwork, filling your space with plants and natural elements, or creating a dedicated play area with toys and games.

Invite spontaneity into your daily routine by leaving room for unstructured play and exploration. Set aside time each day to indulge in creative pursuits without a specific agenda or goal in mind. Allow yourself to follow your whims and explore new ideas without judgment or expectation.

Embracing Curiosity and Wonder

Cultivate a sense of curiosity and wonder by approaching each day with a sense of openness and receptivity. Allow yourself to be fascinated by the world around you, finding beauty and inspiration in the ordinary. Take time to notice the small miracles of life – the delicate intricacies of a flower, the mesmerizing patterns in a snowflake, the rhythm of your own breath.

Ask questions and seek answers with the curiosity of a child. Embrace the unknown and be willing to explore new ideas and perspectives. Allow yourself to be surprised and delighted by the wonders of the universe, and cultivate a sense of awe and reverence for the mysteries of life.

In conclusion, rekindling your inner child is essential for unleashing your creative genius. By reconnecting with your playful imagination, incorporating elements of play into your daily life, embracing the joy of learning, finding humor and lightheartedness in the creative process, practicing mindfulness and presence, creating a playful environment, and embracing curiosity and wonder, you can tap into the boundless creativity of your youthful self. So, embrace your inner child, let go of inhibitions, and rediscover the joy of creativity and imagination.

Chapter 04

The Power of Constraints

Constraints are often viewed as barriers to creativity, imposing limitations and restrictions on our ability to innovate. However, paradoxically, it's within these constraints that creativity flourishes most profoundly. In this chapter, we'll explore the transformative power of constraints and how embracing limitations can fuel our creative endeavors.

Shifting Your Perspective on Limitations

To harness the power of constraints, it's essential to shift your perspective on limitations. Rather than seeing them as obstacles, view constraints as opportunities for creativity. Constraints force us to think more deeply, to innovate, and to find alternative solutions. They challenge us to work within specific boundaries, pushing the boundaries of our creativity in the process.

Instead of viewing constraints as limitations, reframe them as parameters that guide and shape our creative process. Embrace the challenge of working within constraints, recognizing that they can lead to unexpected discoveries and breakthroughs.

Consider the story of the French chef Auguste Escoffier, who famously said, "Good cuisine is the result of constraints and a respect for tradition." Escoffier understood that constraints, such as seasonal ingredients and culinary traditions, are essential ingredients in the creative process. By working within these constraints, chefs can create innovative dishes that celebrate the flavors and traditions of their culture.

Working Within Specific Boundaries

Working within specific boundaries, whether they are time constraints, budget limitations, or material restrictions, can spark ingenuity and resourcefulness. When faced with constraints, we're forced to prioritize, focus our efforts, and make the most of what we have.

For example, consider the concept of "creative constraints" in art and design. By imposing limitations on color palette, materials, or composition, artists can push the boundaries of their creativity and produce innovative works of art. Constraints provide a framework within which creativity can thrive, guiding the creative process and sparking new ideas.

Architects, too, are familiar with the power of constraints. When designing a building, they must consider factors such as site conditions, building codes, and client preferences. These constraints shape the design process, guiding architects to create buildings that are not only functional but also aesthetically pleasing and environmentally sustainable.

Encouraging "Out-of-the-Box" Thinking

Constraints often require us to think "outside the box" and explore unconventional solutions to problems. When faced with limitations, challenge yourself to approach the problem from a different angle, question assumptions, and consider alternative perspectives.

For example, consider the story of Swiss engineer George de Mestral, who was inspired to invent Velcro after observing how burrs stuck to his dog's fur during a walk in the woods. By recognizing the potential of this natural phenomenon and thinking creatively about how it could be applied, de Mestral developed one of the most iconic fastening systems in history.

Similarly, the Japanese art of origami demonstrates the power of constraints to inspire creativity. By folding a single sheet of paper according to a set of rules and limitations, origami artists can create intricate sculptures and designs that captivate the imagination. The constraints of origami – a square sheet of paper, no cutting or tearing – encourage artists to explore new possibilities and push the boundaries of their creativity.

Learning from Historical Examples

Throughout history, artists, inventors, and innovators have thrived under constraints, producing groundbreaking work in the face of adversity. Consider the story of Vincent van Gogh, who created some of his most iconic masterpieces during periods of intense personal struggle and financial hardship.

Or take the example of the Apollo 13 mission, which faced near-catastrophic failure when an oxygen tank exploded en route to the moon. Through ingenuity, teamwork, and creative problem-solving, NASA engineers devised innovative solutions to bring the astronauts safely back to Earth.

The story of the Eiffel Tower provides another compelling example of creativity under constraints. When Gustave Eiffel was commissioned to design a centerpiece for the 1889 World's Fair in Paris, he faced numerous challenges, including limited time and budget constraints. Despite these limitations, Eiffel and his team created an iconic structure that has become a symbol of innovation and engineering excellence.

Applying Constraints to Your Creative Process

Incorporating constraints into your creative process can unlock new levels of innovation and inspiration. Start by identifying the specific constraints you're facing, whether they are external limitations imposed by time, budget, or resources, or internal barriers such as self-doubt or perfectionism.

Next, embrace these constraints as catalysts for creativity. Instead of seeing them as roadblocks, view them as opportunities to think creatively and find novel solutions. Experiment with different approaches, challenge yourself to push beyond your comfort zone, and embrace the unexpected twists and turns of the creative journey.

Consider setting specific constraints or challenges for yourself as a way to stimulate creativity. For example, give yourself a time limit to complete a task, restrict yourself to a limited palette of materials, or impose a ban on certain technologies or tools. By embracing constraints and working within specific boundaries, you can unlock new possibilities and unleash your full creative potential.

Creating a Playful Environment

Design your living or workspace to reflect your playful spirit and inspire creativity. Surround yourself with colors, textures, and objects that spark joy and ignite your imagination. Incorporate elements of whimsy and fun into your environment, whether it's decorating with vibrant artwork, filling your space with plants and natural elements, or creating a dedicated play area with toys and games.

Invite spontaneity into your daily routine by leaving room for unstructured play and exploration. Set aside time each day to indulge in creative pursuits without a specific agenda or goal in mind. Allow yourself to follow your whims and explore new ideas without judgment or expectation.

Embracing Curiosity and Wonder

Cultivate a sense of curiosity and wonder by approaching each day with a sense of openness and receptivity. Allow yourself to be fascinated by the world around you, finding beauty and inspiration in the ordinary. Take time to notice the small miracles of life – the delicate intricacies of a flower, the mesmerizing patterns in a snowflake, the rhythm of your own breath.

Ask questions and seek answers with the curiosity of a child. Embrace the unknown and be willing to explore new ideas and perspectives. Allow yourself to be surprised and delighted by the wonders of the universe, and cultivate a sense of awe and reverence for the mysteries of life.

In conclusion, rekindling your inner child is essential for unleashing your creative genius. By reconnecting with your playful imagination, incorporating elements of play into your daily life, embracing the joy of learning, finding humor and lightheartedness in the creative process, practicing mindfulness and presence, creating a playful environment, and embracing curiosity and wonder, you can tap into the boundless creativity of your youthful self. So, embrace your inner child, let go of inhibitions, and rediscover the joy of creativity and imagination.

Chapter 05

Embracing the Messy Middle

Creativity is often romanticized as a smooth and linear journey from inspiration to realization. However, the reality is far messier. The creative process is filled with twists and turns, setbacks and breakthroughs, moments of doubt and triumph. In this chapter, we'll explore the importance of embracing the messy middle—the turbulent and uncertain phases of creativity—and how to navigate them with resilience and grace.

Understanding the Nonlinear Nature of Creativity

Creativity is rarely a linear process. Instead, it resembles a tangled web of ideas, iterations, and revisions. Expect detours and deviations from your original plan. Embrace the chaos and uncertainty as essential components of the creative journey.

The messy middle is where the magic happens—the space between conception and completion where ideas take shape and evolve. It's where you wrestle with doubt and uncertainty, where breakthroughs emerge from the depths of chaos. Embrace the messiness of creativity, knowing that it's all part of the process.

Consider the story of J.K. Rowling, who famously wrote the first Harry Potter book in cafes while struggling to make ends meet as a single mother. Rowling faced numerous rejections before finally finding a publisher willing to take a chance on her manuscript. Her journey is a testament to the nonlinear nature of creativity and the importance of perseverance in the face of adversity.

Accepting "Good Enough"

Perfectionism is the enemy of creativity. Striving for perfection often leads to paralysis, preventing you from taking risks and exploring new possibilities. Instead, embrace the concept of "good enough." Recognize that perfection is elusive and subjective, and that sometimes, good enough is all you need to move forward.

"Good enough" is not about settling for mediocrity; it's about recognizing when a project has reached a point of diminishing returns. It's about prioritizing progress over perfection and trusting in your ability to refine and improve your work over time.

In his book "Art & Fear," David Bayles and Ted Orland discuss the concept of the "good enough" potter. They describe an experiment where one group of students was graded solely on the quantity of work they produced, while another group was graded solely on the quality of their work. Surprisingly, the group graded on quantity produced higher-quality work. This experiment illustrates the importance of embracing imperfection and focusing on the process rather than the outcome.

Learning to Persevere

Creative slumps and moments of self-doubt are inevitable on the creative journey. The key is to persevere—to keep pushing forward even when the path ahead seems uncertain. Remember that creativity is not always about inspiration; it's about dedication and hard work.

When you find yourself facing a creative block, don't give up. Instead, lean into the discomfort and explore new avenues of inspiration. Take a break if you need to, but don't let fear or doubt hold you back. Trust in your creative process and believe in your ability to overcome obstacles.

Author Elizabeth Gilbert discusses the concept of "stubborn gladness" in her book "Big Magic." She encourages creatives to persist in their work even when faced with rejection or failure. Gilbert believes that the act of creating is inherently joyful and that stubbornly pursuing your creative passions, despite setbacks, is an act of defiance against the forces that seek to stifle your creativity.

Developing a Growth Mindset

Central to embracing the messy middle is cultivating a growth mindset—a belief that your abilities and intelligence can be developed through dedication and hard work. Embrace challenges as opportunities for growth and learning. Celebrate mistakes as valuable lessons on the path to mastery.

Rather than viewing setbacks as failures, see them as feedback—signposts guiding you toward greater understanding and insight. Approach your creative endeavors with a sense of curiosity and openness, knowing that every experience, whether positive or negative, contributes to your growth and development.

Psychologist Carol Dweck popularized the concept of the growth mindset in her book "Mindset: The New Psychology of Success." She argues that individuals with a growth mindset are more resilient in the face of challenges and more likely to persevere in the pursuit of their goals. By embracing a growth mindset, you can navigate the messy middle with confidence and resilience.

Celebrating Incremental Progress

In the messy middle, progress is often incremental— small victories accumulated over time. Learn to celebrate these milestones, no matter how small. Recognize the value of progress, however modest, and use it as fuel to propel you forward.

Keep a journal or progress tracker to document your achievements and milestones. Celebrate each step forward, no matter how insignificant it may seem. By acknowledging your progress, you reinforce your commitment to your creative goals and build momentum toward success.

In his book "The Progress Principle," Harvard professor Teresa Amabile discusses the importance of small wins in fueling creativity and motivation. She found that employees who experienced frequent small wins in their work reported higher levels of motivation, engagement, and creativity. By celebrating incremental progress, you can maintain momentum and stay motivated during the messy middle of the creative process.

Finding Joy in the Process

Above all, find joy in the process of creation. Embrace the messiness, the uncertainty, and the imperfection. Take pleasure in the act of making, knowing that each brushstroke, each word, each note brings you one step closer to realizing your vision.

Remember that creativity is not just about the end result; it's about the journey — the ups and downs, the twists and turns, the moments of frustration and exhilaration. Embrace the messiness of creativity, knowing that it's all part of the rich tapestry of human experience.

In conclusion, embracing the messy middle is essential for navigating the creative journey with resilience and grace. By understanding the nonlinear nature of creativity, accepting "good enough," learning to persevere through creative slumps, developing a growth mindset, celebrating incremental progress, and finding joy in the process, you can navigate the messy middle with confidence and emerge stronger and more resilient on the other side. So, embrace the messiness, trust in your creative process, and let the journey unfold one messy step at a time.

Chapter 06

The Inspiration Playground

Creativity thrives in an environment rich with inspiration. In this chapter, we'll explore the significance of cultivating an inspiration playground—a space where ideas can flourish and creativity can thrive. From actively seeking out inspiration to surrounding yourself with stimulating influences, we'll delve into the various ways you can nurture your creative spirit and fuel your imagination.

Actively Seeking Out Inspiration

Inspiration is everywhere, waiting to be discovered. Actively seeking out sources of inspiration can ignite your creativity and spark new ideas. Whether it's exploring art galleries, immersing yourself in nature, or listening to music, expose yourself to a diverse range of stimuli to fuel your imagination.

Visit museums and galleries to discover works of art that resonate with you. Pay attention to the colors, textures, and compositions that catch your eye, and allow them to inspire your own creative pursuits. Take walks in nature to observe the beauty and intricacy of the natural world. Notice the patterns in the leaves, the play of light and shadow, and the sounds of the forest. Nature has a way of sparking creativity and instilling a sense of wonder and awe.

Listen to music that moves you emotionally and intellectually. Pay attention to the melodies, rhythms, and lyrics that evoke powerful emotions or transport you to another world. Music has the power to inspire creativity and unlock new realms of imagination.

Engage with literature and poetry that speaks to your soul. Explore works of fiction, non-fiction, and poetry that challenge your perceptions and expand your worldview. Allow yourself to be transported to different times and places, and draw inspiration from the rich tapestry of human experience.

Experiment with different forms of media and entertainment, such as film, television, and theater. Explore stories, characters, and themes that resonate with you, and consider how they might inform your own creative projects.

Creating a Dedicated "Inspiration Board"

One way to capture and organize your sources of inspiration is to create a dedicated "inspiration board." Gather images, quotes, and other visual elements that resonate with you and arrange them on a bulletin board or digital collage. Use this board as a visual reference to spark creativity and remind yourself of the ideas and themes that inspire you.

Include photographs, illustrations, and artwork that inspire you creatively. Choose images that evoke a mood or convey a message that resonates with your own artistic vision. Incorporate quotes and excerpts from books, poems, or speeches that inspire you to think differently or challenge your assumptions. Surround yourself with visuals and words that ignite your imagination and fuel your creative fire.

Consider creating a digital inspiration board using platforms like Pinterest or Trello, where you can easily collect and organize images, articles, and other online resources. Use tags and categories to group similar ideas and themes, making it easy to navigate and explore your inspiration.

Surrounding Yourself with Creative People

Creativity thrives in a supportive community of like-minded individuals. Surround yourself with creative people who share your passion for innovation and exploration. Engage in stimulating conversations, exchange ideas, and collaborate on projects that inspire you.

Join creative communities, such as art collectives, writing groups, or maker spaces, where you can connect with other artists and creators. Attend workshops, classes, and networking events to expand your circle of creative contacts and learn from others' experiences. Surround yourself with people who challenge and inspire you to reach new heights of creativity.

Seek out mentors and role models who have achieved success in your field of interest. Learn from their experiences, ask for advice, and draw inspiration from their achievements. Surround yourself with positive influences who support and encourage your creative endeavors.

Practicing Mindfulness

Practicing mindfulness can help you cultivate a deeper awareness of your surroundings and allow yourself to be present for unexpected inspiration. Take time each day to quiet your mind, focus on your breath, and observe the world around you with open curiosity.

Engage your senses fully in each moment, noticing the sights, sounds, smells, and sensations that surround you. Allow yourself to be fully present for the beauty and wonder of the world, without judgment or distraction. Mindfulness can help you cultivate a receptive mindset and create space for creativity to flourish.

Incorporate mindfulness practices into your daily routine, such as meditation, yoga, or mindful walking. Set aside dedicated time each day to engage in these activities and cultivate a sense of presence and awareness. Use mindfulness techniques to quiet your inner critic, calm your mind, and open yourself up to new ideas and inspiration.

Exploring New Experiences

Embrace novelty and exploration as a way to stimulate creativity and fuel your imagination. Step outside your comfort zone and seek out new experiences that challenge your assumptions and broaden your perspective.

Travel to new destinations and immerse yourself in different cultures and environments. Explore unfamiliar landscapes, taste exotic cuisines, and engage with locals to gain new insights and inspiration. Traveling opens your mind to new possibilities and fuels your creativity by exposing you to new sights, sounds, and experiences.

Experiment with different hobbies and activities to spark your creativity and expand your skill set. Take up painting, photography, cooking, or gardening — anything that allows you to express yourself creatively and engage your senses fully. Trying new things keeps your mind sharp and flexible, and opens up new avenues of inspiration and discovery.

Conclusion

In conclusion, the inspiration playground is a vital space for nurturing creativity and fueling the imagination. By actively seeking out inspiration from various sources, creating a dedicated inspiration board, surrounding yourself with creative people, practicing mindfulness, and exploring new experiences, you can cultivate an environment where ideas can flourish and creativity can thrive. So, immerse yourself in the beauty and wonder of the world, and let inspiration be your guide on the creative journey.

Chapter 07

Rethinking Your Routine

Our daily routines play a significant role in shaping our creative output. In this chapter, we'll explore how rethinking your routine can revitalize your creativity, inject new energy into your work, and inspire fresh ideas. From identifying and replacing draining activities to scheduling dedicated creativity time, we'll examine strategies for breaking free from the monotony of routine and embracing the unexpected.

Identifying Routine Activities that Drain Your Creativity

The first step in rethinking your routine is to identify the activities that drain your creativity. These might include mundane tasks, repetitive chores, or mindless distractions that leave you feeling uninspired and depleted.

Take stock of your daily habits and routines, and pay attention to how each activity makes you feel. Notice which activities leave you feeling energized and engaged, and which ones leave you feeling drained and uninspired. Be honest with yourself about the impact of these activities on your creativity.

Once you've identified the activities that drain your creativity, look for ways to replace them with more stimulating alternatives. This might involve outsourcing repetitive tasks, streamlining your workflow, or setting boundaries around time-consuming distractions. By freeing up time and energy for more creative pursuits, you can reclaim control over your routine and cultivate a more conducive environment for innovation.

For example, if you find that checking email first thing in the morning leaves you feeling overwhelmed and distracted, consider implementing a "no-email" rule for the first hour of your day. Use this time instead for creative activities such as journaling, brainstorming, or working on a passion project. By prioritizing your creative energy in the morning, you can set a positive tone for the rest of your day.

Breaking Free from Routine

Breaking free from routine is essential for sparking creativity and inspiring new ideas. Instead of following the same predictable patterns day in and day out, challenge yourself to shake things up and embrace the unexpected.

Take different routes to familiar destinations, try new activities, and explore new places. By stepping outside your comfort zone and exposing yourself to new experiences, you can stimulate your mind and awaken your creativity.

Consider the story of author J.R.R. Tolkien, who famously wrote the first line of "The Hobbit" on a blank page of an exam paper while grading exams. Tolkien's willingness to break free from routine and seize unexpected opportunities led to the creation of one of the most beloved works of fantasy literature in history.

To incorporate more spontaneity into your routine, try introducing small changes into your daily life. This could be as simple as rearranging your workspace, trying a new recipe for dinner, or taking a different route on your daily walk. By embracing novelty and unpredictability, you can inject new energy into your routine and spark fresh ideas.

Scheduling Dedicated "Creativity Time"

Incorporating dedicated "creativity time" into your daily routine is essential for nurturing your creative spirit and fostering innovation. Set aside time each day for focused brainstorming, exploration, and experimentation.

Create a dedicated space for creativity where you can escape distractions and immerse yourself in the creative process. Set clear boundaries around this time and communicate your intentions to others to minimize interruptions.

Experiment with different creative techniques and exercises to stimulate your imagination and generate new ideas. Try free writing, mind mapping, or visual brainstorming to unlock your creativity and overcome creative blocks.

Consider setting aside a specific time each day for creativity, such as the first hour of your morning or the last hour before bed. By establishing a consistent routine for creativity, you can train your brain to associate this time with focused creative work and make it a regular part of your daily schedule.

Experimenting with Different Environments

The environment in which you work plays a significant role in shaping your creative output. Experiment with different environments to find the ones that inspire and energize you the most.

Consider working outdoors in nature, where fresh air and natural beauty can stimulate your senses and fuel your creativity. Alternatively, visit museums, galleries, or other cultural institutions to immerse yourself in art and culture and draw inspiration from the works of others.

Coffee shops and cafes can also provide a conducive environment for creativity, with their ambient noise and relaxed atmosphere. The buzz of conversation and the aroma of freshly brewed coffee can create a stimulating backdrop for brainstorming and exploration.

Experiment with different workspaces within your home or office to find the environment that best supports your creative process. Some people thrive in a clean and organized space, while others prefer a more cluttered and eclectic environment. Find what works best for you and tailor your workspace to optimize your creativity.

Conclusion

In conclusion, rethinking your routine is essential for

revitalizing your creativity and inspiring fresh ideas. By identifying and replacing draining activities, breaking free from routine, scheduling dedicated creativity time, and experimenting with different environments, you can create a more conducive environment for innovation and discovery. So, challenge yourself to shake up your routine, embrace the unexpected, and cultivate a creative mindset that embraces change and exploration.

Chapter 08

The Power of Collaboration

Collaboration stands as a cornerstone of creativity, a conduit through which diverse minds converge, ideas intermingle, and innovation flourishes. In this chapter, we delve deeper into the profound impact of collaboration, examining how the fusion of diverse perspectives, the cultivation of creative networks, the art of effective brainstorming, and the collective wisdom garnered from shared experiences can catalyze extraordinary creative endeavors.

Understanding the Power of Diverse Perspectives

At the heart of collaboration lies the potent brew of diverse perspectives. When individuals from disparate backgrounds, cultures, and disciplines unite, they bring with them a tapestry of experiences, insights, and ideas. This amalgamation of perspectives serves as fertile ground for creative exploration, challenging conventional thinking and opening new pathways to innovation.

Consider the field of architecture, where collaboration between architects, engineers, urban planners, and stakeholders is essential for designing spaces that meet the needs of diverse communities. By integrating input from various stakeholders, architects can create buildings and environments that are not only functional and aesthetically pleasing but also responsive to the unique needs and preferences of the people who inhabit them.

Building a Network of Creative Individuals

Central to the collaborative process is the cultivation of a robust network of creative individuals—a collective of minds that inspire and challenge one another to reach new heights of creativity. Surrounding oneself with fellow innovators, mentors, and collaborators fosters a culture of creative exchange, where ideas are freely shared, refined, and expanded upon.

Forge connections with individuals whose perspectives and skills complement your own, seeking out mentors who can offer guidance and support on your creative journey. Attend workshops, conferences, and networking events to expand your circle of creative contacts and immerse yourself in a community of like-minded individuals.

In the digital age, online communities and social media platforms provide fertile ground for connecting with fellow creatives from around the globe. Participate in online forums, join virtual communities, and engage in collaborative projects to tap into a vast reservoir of creative inspiration and expertise.

Engaging in Brainstorming Sessions

Brainstorming sessions serve as crucibles of creativity, where ideas are born, nurtured, and refined through collaborative exploration. By assembling a diverse group of individuals with unique perspectives and expertise, brainstorming sessions unleash a torrent of creative energy, propelling participants toward innovative solutions to complex problems.

When embarking on a brainstorming session, foster an environment of openness, trust, and mutual respect, where all ideas are welcomed and valued. Encourage participants to suspend judgment, embrace ambiguity, and explore unconventional possibilities without fear of criticism or rejection.

Employ techniques such as mind mapping, free association, and role-playing to stimulate creative thinking and spark new connections. Encourage participants to build upon one another's ideas, leveraging the collective creativity of the group to generate a wealth of innovative solutions.

Learning from the Combined Knowledge and Experiences of Others

Collaboration offers a unique opportunity to tap into the collective wisdom and experiences of others, enriching the creative process with insights and perspectives that transcend individual capabilities. By working together on projects, sharing ideas, and exchanging feedback, collaborators leverage each other's strengths and expertise to achieve shared goals and objectives.

Consider the realm of scientific research, where collaboration between researchers from different disciplines accelerates the pace of discovery and innovation. By pooling their resources, expertise, and insights, interdisciplinary teams can tackle complex challenges, break new ground, and push the boundaries of knowledge in their respective fields.

In the creative industries, collaboration often takes the form of interdisciplinary projects that blend art, technology, and storytelling to create immersive experiences that captivate and inspire audiences. From interactive installations to multimedia performances, these collaborative endeavors harness the combined talents of artists, designers, engineers, and storytellers to create something truly extraordinary.

Conclusion

In conclusion, the power of collaboration lies in its ability to harness the collective creativity of diverse individuals, fostering innovation, and unlocking new possibilities. By embracing diverse perspectives, building creative networks, engaging in effective brainstorming sessions, and learning from the combined knowledge and experiences of others, collaborators can create something truly unique and transformative. So, embrace the power of collaboration, seek out opportunities to collaborate with others, and harness the collective creativity of the group to unleash your full creative potential.

Part 2: Cultivating Your Creative Arsenal

Chapter 09
The Magic of Mind Maps

In the vast landscape of creativity, mind maps stand out as versatile tools, capable of unleashing the full potential of the human mind. In this chapter, we embark on a journey into the realm of mind maps, exploring their role as powerful visual brainstorming aids for organizing ideas, fostering innovation, and fueling creative endeavors.

Introducing Mind Maps

At its core, a mind map is a graphical representation of ideas, concepts, and connections, radiating outward from a central theme or topic. Unlike traditional linear note-taking methods, which can feel restrictive and inhibiting, mind maps embrace the fluidity and interconnectedness of thought, allowing for the free-flowing exploration of ideas.

The central idea serves as the focal point of the mind map, branching out into subtopics, key concepts, and related associations. By visually mapping out the connections between various elements, mind maps provide a holistic view of a subject, facilitating deeper understanding, creative insight, and innovative problem-solving.

The beauty of mind maps lies in their ability to capture the nonlinear nature of thought, reflecting the way our minds naturally organize and process information. By embracing this organic approach to idea generation, mind maps encourage creativity, spontaneity, and exploration, empowering individuals to unlock new insights and perspectives.

Learning How to Use Mind Maps

Using mind maps is a straightforward process that requires nothing more than a blank sheet of paper and a willingness to explore. Begin by identifying a central theme or topic that you wish to explore, and write it down in the center of the page. This central node serves as the anchor for your mind map, around which all other ideas will revolve.

Next, start brainstorming ideas related to the central theme, jotting them down as branches radiating outward from the central node. Use keywords, phrases, or images to represent each idea, keeping your thoughts concise and focused. As new ideas emerge, continue branching out from existing nodes, creating a web of interconnected concepts and associations.

As you build your mind map, don't be afraid to follow unexpected tangents or explore seemingly unrelated ideas. The beauty of mind maps lies in their ability to capture the full spectrum of thought, embracing the diversity and complexity of human cognition.

To illustrate, let's consider a hypothetical scenario where you're planning a vacation. You might start by writing "Vacation" in the center of your mind map and then branch out to explore different aspects of your trip, such as destination options, activities, accommodation choices, and travel logistics. Each of these branches can further expand into subtopics, such as specific attractions to visit, local cuisine to try, or transportation options to consider.

Creating Mind Maps for Specific Purposes

Mind maps can be employed for a wide range of purposes, from brainstorming new projects to organizing complex information and setting personal goals. Whether you're embarking on a creative endeavor, planning a project, or seeking clarity on a complex problem, mind maps provide a flexible framework for organizing your thoughts and sparking innovation.

For example, if you're brainstorming ideas for a new product or service, you might create a mind map to explore potential features, target markets, and competitive advantages. By visually mapping out these key elements, you can gain insights into the viability of your ideas and identify areas for further exploration.

Similarly, if you're grappling with a complex problem or decision, you can use a mind map to break down the issue into its component parts, identify potential solutions, and evaluate their respective merits. By mapping out the various factors and considerations involved, you can gain clarity on the best course of action and make more informed decisions.

In the realm of personal development, mind maps can be powerful tools for setting goals, charting progress, and visualizing aspirations. Whether you're planning your career path, outlining a fitness regimen, or mapping out your long-term aspirations, mind maps provide a structured yet flexible framework for articulating your vision and defining actionable steps to achieve your objectives.

Using Mind Maps Collaboratively

One of the most powerful aspects of mind maps is their ability to facilitate collaborative brainstorming and idea generation. By engaging in group mind mapping sessions, teams can harness the collective creativity of their members, generate a wealth of ideas, and build upon each other's thoughts.

Collaborative mind mapping sessions can take various forms, from in-person workshops and brainstorming sessions to virtual collaborations using dedicated mind mapping software or online collaboration tools. Regardless of the format, the key is to create a supportive and inclusive environment where all participants feel empowered to contribute and explore ideas freely.

To illustrate, imagine a team of designers tasked with brainstorming ideas for a new product. They might gather in a conference room, armed with markers and a large whiteboard, and begin collaboratively mapping out their ideas. As one team member suggests a feature or concept, another might build upon it, branching out to explore related ideas or potential applications.

In virtual collaborations, team members can use dedicated mind mapping software or online platforms to collaborate in real-time, regardless of their physical location. These tools allow participants to contribute ideas, add annotations, and make edits to the mind map simultaneously, creating a dynamic and interactive environment for brainstorming and idea generation.

Conclusion

In conclusion, mind maps are powerful tools for organizing ideas, fostering innovation, and fueling creative endeavors. By embracing the fluidity and interconnectedness of thought, mind maps provide a flexible framework for exploring complex topics, generating new ideas, and solving problems creatively. Whether used individually or collaboratively, mind maps offer a visual and intuitive approach to creativity that can unleash the full potential of the human mind. So, pick up a pen and paper, or fire up your favorite mind mapping software, and let your ideas flow freely as you embark on your mind mapping journey.

Chapter 10

The Art of Reframing

In the ever-evolving landscape of creativity, the art of reframing emerges as a masterful stroke, capable of transforming the mundane into the extraordinary and unveiling new dimensions of possibility. In this chapter, we embark on a journey into the transformative realm of reframing, exploring its profound impact on problem-solving, innovation, and creative thinking.

Introducing Reframing

Reframing is a cognitive technique that involves shifting perspectives, altering perceptions, and reinterpreting situations from different angles. It challenges the rigid structures of conventional thinking, inviting us to explore the infinite nuances of our perceptions and assumptions. At its essence, reframing is about embracing the fluidity of thought, breaking free from established patterns, and opening ourselves to new possibilities.

The power of reframing lies in its ability to uncover hidden opportunities, reframe limitations as strengths, and transform seemingly insurmountable challenges into stepping stones for growth. By reframing our perspective, we can navigate uncertainty with clarity, embrace change with resilience, and cultivate a mindset of endless curiosity and exploration.

Applying Reframing to Challenges and Limitations

One of the most profound applications of reframing

lies in its ability to transform challenges and limitations into catalysts for innovation and growth. Instead of viewing obstacles as insurmountable barriers, reframing allows us to see them as opportunities for creative problem-solving and personal development.

For example, imagine you're faced with a tight deadline for a project at work. Instead of succumbing to the pressure and stress, reframing the deadline as a challenge can ignite a sense of urgency and focus. By viewing the deadline as a catalyst for creativity and innovation, you can tap into a reservoir of untapped potential and harness it to meet and exceed expectations.

Similarly, reframing personal limitations as opportunities for growth and self-discovery can unlock new pathways to success. Whether it's overcoming a fear of failure, embracing uncertainty, or confronting imposter syndrome, reframing allows us to view these obstacles through a lens of empowerment and resilience. By reframing limitations as opportunities for learning and growth, we can cultivate a mindset of continuous improvement and achieve our full potential.

Practicing "Reverse Brainstorming"

Reverse brainstorming is a creative technique that flips the traditional brainstorming process on its head, encouraging us to intentionally generate bad ideas as a means of sparking innovative solutions. By challenging conventional thinking and embracing absurdity, reverse brainstorming invites us to explore the outer edges of possibility and uncover hidden insights that may lie beneath the surface.

To practice reverse brainstorming, start by identifying the problem or challenge you're facing. Then, instead of brainstorming ideas to solve the problem, brainstorm ideas that would exacerbate the problem or make it worse. Embrace humor, absurdity, and creativity as you generate bad ideas, allowing yourself to explore unconventional solutions and challenge ingrained assumptions.

Once you've generated a list of bad ideas, examine them critically and look for hidden opportunities or insights that may emerge. Often, the process of exploring bad ideas can lead to unexpected breakthroughs and innovative solutions that may not have been considered otherwise. By embracing the spirit of experimentation and curiosity, reverse brainstorming empowers us to think outside the box and uncover novel solutions to complex problems.

Developing the Ability to Think Metaphorically

Metaphorical thinking is another powerful tool for reframing perspectives and unlocking creative insights. By drawing parallels between seemingly unrelated concepts, we can uncover hidden connections, stimulate our imagination, and gain new insights into familiar problems or ideas.

For example, consider the metaphor of a journey to

represent the process of personal growth and development. By reframing challenges as opportunities to embark on a new adventure, we can approach them with a sense of curiosity and excitement, rather than fear or apprehension. By viewing setbacks as detours on the road to success, we can maintain a sense of perspective and resilience in the face of adversity.

Conclusion

In conclusion, the art of reframing is a powerful tool for unlocking creativity, fostering innovation, and navigating the complexities of the human experience. Whether applied to challenges, limitations, or seemingly bad ideas, reframing invites us to see the world through a different lens, embracing the richness and complexity of our perceptions and assumptions. By practicing techniques such as reverse brainstorming and metaphorical thinking, we can expand our creative horizons, challenge our assumptions, and tap into the boundless potential of the human mind. So, embrace the art of reframing, and watch as new possibilities unfold before your eyes, transforming the ordinary into the extraordinary with each shift in perspective.

Chapter 11

Design Thinking for Innovation

In the ever-evolving landscape of creativity and problem-solving, design thinking stands as a beacon of innovation. In this chapter, we delve into the intricacies of design thinking, exploring its fundamental principles and practical applications in driving creativity, fostering collaboration, and unlocking breakthrough solutions.

Understanding the Core Principles of Design Thinking

At its essence, design thinking is a human-centered approach to problem-solving that prioritizes empathy, collaboration, and iteration. It provides a structured framework for tackling complex challenges and driving innovation by placing the needs and experiences of users at the forefront of the design process. The core principles of design thinking are encapsulated in five key stages: Empathize, Define, Ideate, Prototype, and Test.

1. **Empathize:** The Empathize stage serves as the foundation of the design thinking process, emphasizing the importance of understanding the needs, motivations, and aspirations of users. Through immersive research methods such as interviews, observations, and empathy exercises, design thinkers seek to gain deep insights into the lived experiences of their target audience. By empathizing with users, teams can develop a deep understanding of their pain points, preferences, and unmet needs, laying the groundwork for informed decision-making and

creative problem-solving.

2. **Define:** In the Define stage, design thinkers distill their research findings into actionable insights and define the problem statement or challenge they aim to address. This stage involves synthesizing user data, identifying patterns and themes, and framing the problem in a way that inspires innovative solutions. By clearly defining the problem statement, teams can align their efforts, focus their creativity, and ensure that their solutions are rooted in user needs and aspirations.

3. **Ideate:** The Ideate stage is a brainstorming phase where teams generate a wide range of creative ideas and explore innovative solutions to the defined problem. By embracing a spirit of curiosity, openness, and collaboration, design thinkers can unleash their creativity and push the boundaries of conventional thinking. Techniques such as brainstorming, mind mapping, and rapid sketching are employed to foster ideation and generate diverse perspectives. The goal is to explore a breadth of possibilities, suspend judgment, and cultivate a culture of experimentation and exploration.

4. **Prototype:** In the Prototype stage, design thinkers transform their ideas into tangible prototypes that can be tested and iterated upon. Prototypes serve as low-fidelity representations of potential solutions, allowing teams to quickly bring their ideas to life and gather feedback from users.

Prototyping may involve creating sketches, wireframes, mockups, or physical models, depending on the nature of the problem and the desired level of fidelity. The key is to create prototypes that are sufficient to communicate the intended concept and gather meaningful feedback from users.

5. **Test:** The Test stage is where design thinkers validate their ideas, gather feedback from users, and refine their solutions based on real-world insights. By testing prototypes with users in real-world contexts, teams can uncover usability issues, identify areas for improvement, and refine their designs iteratively. Testing is an iterative process that informs subsequent rounds of prototyping and refinement, ultimately leading to the development of solutions that meet user needs and deliver meaningful impact. The goal is to create solutions that are intuitive, accessible, and user-friendly, driving adoption and engagement.

Applying Design Thinking to Drive Innovation

Design thinking can be applied to a wide range of challenges and opportunities, from developing new products or services to improving existing systems and processes. By embracing a human-centered approach and prioritizing the needs of users, organizations can unlock new pathways to innovation and create solutions that resonate with their target audience.

For example, consider the case of a financial institution seeking to improve the user experience of its mobile banking app. By applying design thinking principles, the institution may conduct user research to understand the needs and preferences of its customers. Based on these insights, they may redefine the problem statement to focus on enhancing usability and accessibility. Through ideation and prototyping, they may explore innovative features such as personalized financial insights, intuitive navigation, and seamless integration with other financial tools. By testing these prototypes with users and iterating based on feedback, the institution can develop a mobile banking app that meets the needs of its customers and delivers a superior user experience.

Learning to Empathize and Design with Users in Mind

Central to the success of design thinking is the ability to empathize with users and design solutions that meet their needs and preferences. By immersing ourselves in the lived experiences of our target audience, we can gain a deeper understanding of their motivations, aspirations, and pain points, guiding the development of more meaningful and impactful solutions.

To cultivate empathy, design thinkers employ a variety of research methods, including ethnographic research, user interviews, contextual inquiries, and journey mapping. These methods enable teams to step into the shoes of their users, see the world through their eyes, and uncover insights that inform the design process. By designing with users in mind, organizations can create solutions that are intuitive, accessible, and user-friendly, driving adoption and engagement.

Building Rapid Prototypes to Test Ideas Quickly

A hallmark of design thinking is its emphasis on rapid prototyping and iteration. By quickly transforming ideas into tangible prototypes, teams can gather feedback early and often, identify strengths and weaknesses, and refine solutions based on user input. Rapid prototyping reduces the risk of investing time and resources in ideas that may not resonate with users, enabling teams to fail fast and learn quickly.

Prototypes can take various forms, from simple sketches and wireframes to interactive mockups and functional prototypes. The key is to create prototypes that are sufficient to communicate the intended concept and gather feedback from users. Rapid prototyping allows teams to explore multiple design alternatives, test hypotheses, and iterate based on real-world feedback, ultimately leading to the development of solutions that meet user needs and deliver meaningful impact.

Conclusion

In conclusion, design thinking offers a structured approach to innovation that prioritizes empathy, collaboration, and experimentation. By embracing the core principles of design thinking—Empathize, Define, Ideate, Prototype, and Test—organizations can drive innovation, foster creativity, and create solutions that resonate with their target audience. Whether developing new products, services, or experiences, the principles of design thinking can guide teams in solving complex problems, uncovering hidden opportunities, and delivering meaningful value to users. So, embrace the power of design thinking, and let empathy, creativity, and collaboration fuel your journey toward innovation and impact.

Chapter 12

The Power of "Yes, And..." Improvisation

In the ever-evolving landscape of creativity and collaboration, the technique of "Yes, And..." improvisation stands as a beacon of innovation and synergy. In this chapter, we delve deeper into the transformative power of "Yes, And..." improvisation, exploring its principles, applications, and profound impact on fostering creativity, building teams, and unlocking breakthrough solutions.

Introducing the Concept of "Yes, And..." Improvisation

"Yes, And..." improvisation is more than just a technique; it's a mindset—a way of approaching interactions, ideas, and challenges with openness, curiosity, and collaboration. Originating from the world of improvisational theater, "Yes, And..." is a fundamental principle that encourages performers to accept and build upon each other's contributions, creating dynamic and spontaneous scenes without the constraints of a script or predetermined narrative.

At its core, "Yes, And..." involves two simple steps:

1. Yes: Acknowledge and accept the ideas, suggestions, or offers presented by others.
2. And: Add to those ideas, expanding upon them and contributing your own insights, perspectives, or contributions.

By embracing the principle of "Yes, And...",

individuals can create a supportive and inclusive environment where creativity flourishes, ideas flow freely, and collaboration thrives. Whether applied in the context of improvisational theater, brainstorming sessions, or team collaborations, "Yes, And..." improvisation empowers individuals to co-create, innovate, and explore new possibilities together.

Practicing Active Listening and Building Upon Ideas

At the heart of "Yes, And..." improvisation lies the practice of active listening—a skill that involves not only hearing what others say but also understanding their perspectives, intentions, and emotions. Active listening requires individuals to be fully present, attentive, and empathetic, tuning into both verbal and nonverbal cues to gain a deeper understanding of the conversation.

In the context of "Yes, And..." improvisation, active listening serves as the foundation for effective collaboration and co-creation. Instead of merely waiting for their turn to speak, participants actively engage with each other's ideas, building upon them and expanding the conversation in new and unexpected directions. This spirit of affirmation and openness fosters trust, respect, and mutual understanding, laying the groundwork for creative exploration and innovation.

To practice active listening and building upon ideas in

a collaborative setting, individuals can:

- Maintain eye contact and nonverbal cues to demonstrate attentiveness and engagement.
- Paraphrase and summarize others' contributions to ensure clarity and understanding.
- Ask open-ended questions to encourage further exploration and elaboration.
- Validate and affirm others' ideas, even if they diverge from your own perspectives or opinions.

By practicing active listening and building upon the ideas of others, individuals can create a dynamic and inclusive environment where creativity thrives, and innovative solutions emerge.

Using "Yes, And..." to Spark Unexpected Connections

One of the key benefits of "Yes, And..." improvisation is its ability to spark unexpected connections and generate innovative solutions. By embracing the principle of affirmation and building upon each other's contributions, participants can explore new ideas, perspectives, and possibilities that may have otherwise remained undiscovered. The iterative nature of "Yes, And..." encourages experimentation, risk-taking, and exploration, leading to breakthrough insights and creative breakthroughs.

To harness the power of "Yes, And..." to spark

unexpected connections, participants can:

- Embrace ambiguity and uncertainty, viewing them as opportunities for exploration and discovery.
- Encourage divergent thinking by exploring multiple perspectives and considering unconventional ideas.
- Create a safe space for experimentation and risk-taking, where failure is viewed as a natural part of the creative process.
- Emphasize collaboration over competition, fostering a sense of shared ownership and collective responsibility for the outcome.

By embracing the spirit of "Yes, And..." improvisation, participants can break down barriers, transcend traditional boundaries, and unlock new pathways to innovation and creativity.

Encouraging a Playful and Collaborative Environment

Central to the success of "Yes, And..." improvisation is the cultivation of a playful and collaborative environment where all ideas are welcomed and explored. By creating a safe space for experimentation, risk-taking, and creative expression, participants can unleash their full potential and engage in uninhibited exploration of ideas and possibilities. This spirit of playfulness and collaboration fosters a sense of camaraderie, trust, and shared purpose, driving the collective pursuit of innovation and excellence.

To encourage a playful and collaborative environment, facilitators can:

- Establish ground rules that promote active listening, affirmation, and inclusivity.
- Create opportunities for team-building activities and icebreakers to foster trust and camaraderie.
- Encourage participants to step outside their comfort zones and explore new ideas with an open mind.
- Celebrate diversity and encourage participants to embrace their unique perspectives and contributions.

By creating a supportive and nonjudgmental atmosphere, facilitators can empower participants to take risks, express themselves freely, and collaborate with confidence, fostering a culture of creativity and innovation.

Conclusion

In conclusion, the technique of "Yes, And..." improvisation offers a powerful framework for fostering creativity, collaboration, and innovation. By embracing the principles of active listening, affirmation, and building upon the ideas of others, participants can create a dynamic and inclusive environment where creativity flourishes, and breakthrough solutions emerge. Whether applied in the context of improvisational theater, brainstorming sessions, or team collaborations, "Yes, And..." improvisation empowers individuals to explore new ideas, spark unexpected connections, and unleash their full creative potential. So, embrace the power of "Yes, And..." improvisation, and watch as new possibilities unfold before your eyes, transforming ordinary interactions into extraordinary moments of inspiration and discovery.

Chapter 13

Embracing Randomness and Serendipity

In the grand tapestry of creativity, randomness and serendipity often emerge as unexpected yet influential threads. This chapter delves into the profound significance of embracing randomness and serendipity, understanding their roles in the creative process, and harnessing their power to unlock new realms of innovation and discovery.

Understanding the Role of Randomness and Unexpected Encounters

Randomness, characterized by its unpredictability and lack of pattern, is a fundamental aspect of the universe. It manifests in myriad ways, from the chaos of natural phenomena to the spontaneous interactions of everyday life. While randomness may initially appear disruptive or chaotic, it also possesses the potential to inspire creativity, provoke novel insights, and catalyze innovative solutions.

The creative process is inherently dynamic and nonlinear, often unfolding in response to unforeseen circumstances and chance encounters. Randomness injects an element of surprise and unpredictability into the creative journey, prompting individuals to adapt, explore, and innovate in response to unexpected stimuli. By embracing randomness, individuals can tap into a rich reservoir of creative potential, uncovering new ideas, connections, and possibilities that transcend conventional thinking.

Leaving Room for Chance Encounters and Coincidences

In a world governed by schedules, routines, and agendas, it can be tempting to resist or overlook the randomness that surrounds us. However, embracing randomness requires a willingness to relinquish control, step outside our comfort zones, and embrace uncertainty. By creating space for chance encounters and coincidences, individuals open themselves to unexpected opportunities and serendipitous discoveries.

To embrace randomness and serendipity, individuals can:

- Foster a spirit of openness and receptivity to the unexpected, welcoming new experiences and ideas with curiosity and enthusiasm.
- Embrace spontaneity and flexibility, allowing room for serendipitous encounters to unfold organically.
- Cultivate a sense of wonder and awe, recognizing the beauty and mystery inherent in the unpredictable nature of life.
- Trust in the inherent order and intelligence of the universe, believing that random events and coincidences often carry profound meaning and significance.

By embracing randomness and serendipity, individuals can cultivate a sense of adventure, spontaneity, and discovery, leading to unexpected breakthroughs and transformative insights.

Taking Calculated Risks and Stepping Outside Your Comfort Zone

While randomness may introduce an element of uncertainty into the creative process, taking calculated risks and stepping outside one's comfort zone can amplify its transformative potential. By embracing uncertainty and venturing into the unknown, individuals can expand their horizons, challenge their assumptions, and uncover new sources of inspiration and insight.

Taking calculated risks involves assessing the potential rewards and consequences of a decision and making informed choices based on available information. While venturing into uncharted territory may evoke feelings of fear or apprehension, it also offers an opportunity for growth, exploration, and self-discovery. By embracing uncertainty and embracing the unknown, individuals can cultivate resilience, adaptability, and a willingness to embrace the unexpected.

Keeping a Notebook or Recording Device Handy

In the midst of life's unpredictability, it's essential to capture and preserve the insights and inspirations that emerge from random experiences. Keeping a notebook or recording device handy allows individuals to document fleeting thoughts, ideas, and observations sparked by chance encounters and serendipitous discoveries. Whether jotting down a passing thought, sketching a fleeting impression, or recording a snippet of conversation, these artifacts serve as tangible reminders of the creative potential inherent in randomness.

By keeping a notebook or recording device within reach, individuals can transform random experiences into a treasury of creative inspiration and insight. These captured moments serve as a wellspring of ideas, fueling the creative process and igniting new pathways of exploration and discovery. Whether revisiting them in quiet moments of reflection or sharing them with others, these artifacts bear witness to the serendipitous magic of life and the boundless possibilities that arise from embracing randomness.

Conclusion

In conclusion, embracing randomness and serendipity is essential to nurturing creativity, fostering innovation, and cultivating a sense of wonder and possibility. By acknowledging the inherent uncertainty of the creative journey and welcoming the unexpected as a source of inspiration and opportunity, individuals can tap into a vast reservoir of creative potential and unlock new realms of exploration and discovery. Whether encountering chance encounters, coincidences, or serendipitous discoveries, embracing randomness invites individuals to embrace the inherent magic and mystery of life, leading to unexpected breakthroughs and transformative insights. So, embrace the randomness of life, trust in the serendipity of the universe, and allow yourself to be swept away by the currents of creativity and possibility, knowing that the greatest discoveries often lie hidden within the unexpected twists and turns of fate.

Chapter 14

Hacking Your Creativity

In the tumultuous journey of creativity, there are bound to be moments when inspiration wanes and ideas seem elusive. This chapter unveils an arsenal of techniques designed to jumpstart your creativity when faced with the dreaded block. From quick exercises to creative constraints, we explore strategies to reignite the creative flame and unleash a torrent of innovation.

Introducing Various Techniques to Jumpstart Your Creativity

When the creative well runs dry, it's essential to have a toolkit of techniques at your disposal to reignite the spark. From tried-and-true methods to unconventional approaches, there are countless ways to jumpstart your creativity and break through the barriers of mental stagnation.

1. Freewriting

Freewriting is a powerful technique for bypassing the inner critic and tapping into the subconscious mind. Set a timer for a specific duration, such as 10 or 15 minutes, and write continuously without pausing to edit or censor yourself. Let your thoughts flow freely onto the page, exploring different ideas, perspectives, and possibilities without judgment. The goal is to bypass the analytical mind and access the deeper wellspring of creativity that lies beneath the surface.

2. Doodling

Doodling is not just a mindless activity but a powerful tool for stimulating creativity and generating new ideas. Grab a pen and paper and allow your mind to wander as you doodle aimlessly. Embrace the spontaneity of the process, letting your hand move intuitively across the page without worrying about the outcome. Doodling can serve as a gateway to new ideas and insights, tapping into the subconscious mind and unlocking hidden reservoirs of creativity.

3. Timed Brainstorming Sessions

Timed brainstorming sessions are a great way to generate a large number of ideas in a short amount of time. Set a timer for a short duration, such as 5 or 10 minutes, and challenge yourself to generate as many ideas as possible within that timeframe. Embrace quantity over quality, allowing yourself to explore wild and unconventional ideas without self-censorship. The goal is to break through mental barriers and stimulate divergent thinking.

Experimenting with Creative Constraints

Creativity thrives within constraints, as limitations can serve as catalysts for innovation and ingenuity. By imposing specific parameters or restrictions, you can challenge yourself to think outside the box and explore unconventional solutions to creative problems.

1. Using Specific Colors or Materials

Limit your palette to a few select colors or restrict yourself to working with a particular set of materials. By embracing constraints, you force yourself to find creative solutions within the confines of your chosen limitations, leading to unexpected discoveries and breakthroughs.

2. Setting Time Limits

Give yourself a strict deadline to complete a creative task, such as writing a short story in 30 minutes or creating a piece of artwork in an hour. Time constraints can spur productivity and focus, encouraging you to make decisions quickly and trust your instincts.

3. Imposing Structural Limitations

Experiment with different forms or structures, such as writing a sonnet, composing a haiku, or creating a collage. By adhering to established frameworks, you can explore new avenues of expression and push the boundaries of your creativity.

Taking Breaks and Engaging in Mind-Wandering Activities

Creativity thrives in a relaxed and open state of mind, making it essential to take breaks and engage in activities that allow your thoughts to wander freely.

1. Nature Walks

Spend time outdoors, immersing yourself in the sights, sounds, and sensations of the natural world. Nature has a way of rejuvenating the spirit and stimulating creativity, offering a wealth of inspiration and beauty to draw upon.

2. Mindfulness Meditation

Practice mindfulness meditation to cultivate a calm and focused state of mind. By observing your thoughts without judgment and returning to the present moment, you can quiet the chatter of the mind and tap into a deeper wellspring of creativity.

3. Engaging in Playful Activities

Embrace your inner child by engaging in playful activities such as building with blocks, solving puzzles, or playing games. These activities stimulate the imagination and encourage a sense of spontaneity and joy, fostering a fertile ground for creativity to flourish.

Conclusion

In conclusion, hacking your creativity requires a willingness to experiment, play, and embrace the unexpected. By incorporating techniques such as free writing, doodling, and timed brainstorming sessions, you can overcome creative blocks and unleash a torrent of innovation. Likewise, by experimenting with creative constraints and taking breaks to recharge, you can tap into new sources of inspiration and insight. So, arm yourself with these tools and techniques, and watch as your creativity soars to new heights, unlocking hidden reservoirs of potential and possibility along the way.

Chapter 15

Building a Creative Habit

Creativity is not just a fleeting moment of inspiration; it's a muscle that can be strengthened through consistent practice. In this chapter, we delve deeper into the importance of building a creative habit and provide practical strategies for integrating creativity into your daily routine.

Understanding the Importance of Consistency

Consistency is the cornerstone of any creative endeavor. Like a gardener tending to their plants, nurturing your creativity requires regular care and attention. Consistency in creative practice not only fosters skill development but also cultivates a deeper connection to your creative intuition.

Consistency breeds familiarity and comfort with the creative process, allowing you to navigate its twists and turns with confidence and ease. It establishes a rhythm and momentum that propels you forward, even when faced with obstacles or setbacks. Whether it's writing, drawing, or experimenting with new ideas, making creativity a regular part of your life can yield profound results over time.

Integrating Creative Practices into Your Daily Routine

Incorporating creativity into your daily routine doesn't have to be daunting or time-consuming. Even small, incremental steps can have a significant impact on your creative growth. The key is to find opportunities to infuse creativity into your daily life, whether it's during your morning routine, lunch break, or evening wind-down.

Here are some practical ways to integrate creative practices into your daily routine:

- Morning Rituals: Start your day with a creative activity, such as journaling, sketching, or brainstorming ideas. This sets a positive tone for the day ahead and primes your mind for creative thinking.

- Micro-Creativity Breaks: Take short breaks throughout the day to engage in creative activities, such as doodling, writing a haiku, or listening to music. These micro-creativity breaks can provide a refreshing mental reset and stimulate fresh ideas.

- Evening Reflection: Dedicate time in the evening to reflect on your day and capture any creative insights or inspirations that emerged. This reflection practice can help reinforce your creative habits and identify areas for growth.

Setting Realistic Goals

Setting realistic goals is essential for building a sustainable creative habit. Rather than aiming for grandiose achievements, focus on setting small, achievable goals that align with your interests and priorities. This could be as simple as spending 15 minutes each day writing in your journal or completing one sketch per week.

When setting goals, consider the SMART criteria:

- Specific: Clearly define what you want to accomplish.
- Measurable: Identify concrete metrics for tracking your progress.
- Achievable: Ensure that your goals are within reach and realistic.
- Relevant: Align your goals with your values, interests, and long-term aspirations.
- Time-bound: Establish deadlines or timelines for achieving your goals.

By setting realistic goals, you create a roadmap for success and maintain motivation and momentum in your creative practice.

Holding Yourself Accountable

Accountability is a powerful motivator for maintaining a creative habit. Whether it's through self-accountability or external support systems, holding yourself accountable for consistent creative engagement can help you stay on track and overcome procrastination or self-doubt.

Here are some strategies for holding yourself accountable:

- **Daily Check-Ins:** Take a few minutes each day to review your progress and reflect on your creative accomplishments. Celebrate your successes and identify areas for improvement.

- **Accountability Partners:** Find a creative accountability partner or join a community of like-minded individuals who can provide support, encouragement, and feedback. Share your goals and progress with them regularly, and hold each other accountable for staying committed to your creative practice.

- **Public Commitments:** Make your creative goals public by sharing them on social media, writing them down in a journal, or posting them in a visible location. The act of making your intentions public can increase your sense of accountability and commitment to your creative pursuits.

Tracking Your Progress and Celebrating Achievements

Tracking your progress is essential for maintaining momentum and staying motivated in your creative practice. Keep a journal, calendar, or digital tracker to record your daily creative activities, milestones, and insights. This allows you to monitor your growth over time and identify patterns or trends in your creative process.

In addition to tracking your progress, take time to celebrate your achievements along the way. Acknowledge your hard work and dedication, no matter how small, and reward yourself for reaching milestones or accomplishing goals. Celebrating your achievements reinforces positive habits and cultivates a sense of pride and satisfaction in your creative journey.

Conclusion

Building a creative habit is a transformative journey that requires dedication, perseverance, and self-discipline. By understanding the importance of consistency, integrating creative practices into your daily routine, setting realistic goals, holding yourself accountable, and tracking your progress, you can cultivate a sustainable creative practice that fuels your growth and fulfillment.

Remember that creativity is not a destination but a lifelong journey of exploration and discovery. Embrace the process, trust in your instincts, and keep showing up for your creative practice, one day at a time. With patience, persistence, and passion, you can unlock your creative potential and unleash your imagination in ways you never thought possible.

Chapter 16

Sharpening Your Creative Saw

In the pursuit of creativity, one often overlooks the essential foundation upon which it thrives – self-care. This chapter delves into the critical role of nurturing oneself to maintain creative energy and offers comprehensive strategies for sharpening your creative saw.

Emphasizing the Importance of Self-Care

Self-care is a cornerstone of sustained creativity. It is the act of intentionally tending to one's physical, mental, and emotional well-being to ensure optimal functioning and vitality. Just as a well-maintained tool yields better results, nurturing yourself ensures that you can bring your best self to your creative endeavors.

Getting Enough Sleep

Sleep is not merely downtime; it's a critical period of rest and restoration for the body and mind. Adequate sleep is paramount for cognitive function, memory consolidation, and emotional regulation – all essential components of creativity. Aim for 7-9 hours of quality sleep each night, prioritizing consistent sleep and wake times to regulate your body's internal clock.

Eating Healthy Foods

Nutrition is fuel for the body and mind, directly impacting cognitive function and mood. A balanced diet rich in fruits, vegetables, whole grains, lean proteins, and healthy fats provides the nutrients necessary for optimal brain health and creative thinking. Minimize processed foods, sugary snacks, and excessive caffeine intake, as these can lead to energy crashes and hinder mental clarity.

Exercising Regularly

Physical activity is not only beneficial for physical health but also has profound effects on cognitive function and creativity. Regular exercise increases blood flow to the brain, stimulates the release of neurotransmitters like dopamine and serotonin, and reduces stress and anxiety. Incorporate activities you enjoy, such as walking, jogging, yoga, or dancing, aiming for at least 30 minutes of moderate-intensity exercise most days of the week.

Practicing Mindfulness and Meditation

Mindfulness and meditation are potent tools for cultivating presence, reducing stress, and enhancing creativity. These practices involve bringing awareness to the present moment, observing thoughts and sensations without judgment, and cultivating a sense of calm and clarity. Dedicate time each day to mindfulness exercises, such as deep breathing, body scans, or guided meditation, to quiet the mind and nurture inner peace.

Prioritizing Joyful Activities

In the busyness of life, it's easy to neglect activities that bring us joy and replenish our spirit. However, prioritizing these activities is essential for maintaining a sense of balance and fulfillment. Whether it's spending time in nature, engaging in creative pursuits, or connecting with loved ones, make time for activities that nourish your soul and reignite your passion for life.

Cultivating Gratitude

Gratitude is a powerful practice that can transform your outlook on life and enhance your well-being. Take time each day to reflect on the things you're grateful for, whether big or small. Cultivating a mindset of gratitude shifts your focus from scarcity to abundance, fostering a sense of contentment and satisfaction that fuels creativity.

Setting Boundaries

Boundaries are essential for protecting your time, energy, and mental well-being. Learn to say no to commitments that drain your resources and prioritize activities that align with your values and priorities. Establishing clear boundaries allows you to focus on what matters most and create space for creativity to flourish.

Seeking Inspiration

Inspiration is the lifeblood of creativity, fueling the imagination and sparking new ideas. Surround yourself with sources of inspiration, whether it's art, music, literature, or nature. Take time to explore new experiences, visit museums, attend performances, or travel to new places. Exposing yourself to diverse stimuli broadens your perspective and stimulates creativity.

Connecting with Others

Creativity thrives in collaboration and community. Surround yourself with supportive individuals who encourage and inspire your creative pursuits. Seek out opportunities to collaborate with others, share ideas, and receive feedback. Building a network of like-minded individuals fosters a sense of belonging and provides valuable support on your creative journey.

Conclusion

In conclusion, sharpening your creative saw is not a luxury but a necessity for sustaining creativity over the long term. By prioritizing self-care, including adequate sleep, healthy nutrition, regular exercise, mindfulness practices, and joyful activities, you lay the foundation for vibrant creativity and overall well-being.

Remember that self-care is not selfish; it's essential for nurturing your creative spirit and fulfilling your potential. Incorporate these strategies into your daily life, making self-care a non-negotiable priority. By investing in yourself, you not only enhance your creative output but also cultivate a deeper sense of fulfillment and joy in all aspects of life. So, commit to sharpening your creative saw and watch as your creativity flourishes and your life transforms in beautiful and unexpected ways.

Part 3:
Igniting Innovation in Your Life

Chapter 17

Innovation at Work

Innovation is the lifeblood of progress, and it's not limited to tech giants or cutting-edge startups. Every workplace, regardless of its industry or size, can benefit from a culture of innovation. In this chapter, we'll delve into the intricacies of igniting innovation in your current job or professional field, from spotting opportunities to implementing creative solutions, and ultimately, earning recognition as a change maker within your organization.

Identifying Opportunities to Innovate

Innovation often starts with recognizing areas within your organization that could benefit from change or enhancement. This could involve anything from optimizing existing processes and workflows to developing entirely new products or services. To identify these opportunities, keep your eyes and ears open, actively seek feedback from colleagues and customers, and stay abreast of industry trends and best practices.

Consider the following avenues for identifying opportunities to innovate in your workplace:

- Feedback Loops: Actively solicit feedback from colleagues, customers, and stakeholders to gain insights into pain points, unmet needs, and areas for improvement.

- Market Research: Stay informed about industry trends, competitor activities, and emerging technologies through market research and industry publications.

- Cross-Functional Collaboration: Collaborate with colleagues from different departments or disciplines to gain diverse perspectives and identify opportunities for synergy or innovation.

Thinking Creatively About Problem-Solving

Creativity is a potent tool for problem-solving, enabling you to approach challenges from fresh angles and devise innovative solutions. When confronted with a problem at work, resist the urge to default to conventional thinking or rely on past solutions. Instead, unleash your creativity by brainstorming alternative approaches, asking thought-provoking questions, and exploring unconventional avenues for resolution.

Here's how you can cultivate creative problem-solving in your workplace:

- Divergent Thinking: Encourage brainstorming sessions where all ideas are welcome, no matter how unconventional. Embrace divergent thinking, which involves generating a multitude of ideas before converging on the most promising ones.

- Challenge Assumptions: Question existing assumptions, norms, and constraints that may be limiting your thinking. Sometimes, the most innovative solutions emerge when you challenge the status quo and think outside the box.

- Experimentation and Prototyping: Don't be afraid to experiment with new ideas and prototypes, even if they initially seem risky or unorthodox. Embrace a mindset of continuous experimentation and learning from failure.

Process Improvement

Many opportunities for innovation lie in optimizing existing processes and workflows to enhance efficiency, quality, and customer satisfaction. Whether it's streamlining administrative tasks, automating repetitive processes, or reengineering supply chain logistics, there's always room for improvement.

Consider the following strategies for process improvement:

- Root Cause Analysis: Identify the underlying causes of inefficiencies or bottlenecks in your processes through root cause analysis techniques such as the 5 Whys or fishbone diagrams.

- Lean Principles: Apply lean principles such as value stream mapping, Kaizen events, and just-in-time inventory to eliminate waste and streamline workflows.

- Continuous Improvement: Foster a culture of continuous improvement by encouraging employees at all levels to suggest process enhancements and participate in problem-solving initiatives.

Product Development

Innovation in product development involves creating new products or services that address unmet needs, capitalize on market opportunities, or differentiate your organization from competitors. Whether you work in product management, marketing, engineering, or another function, there are ample opportunities to innovate in product development.

Here are some strategies for fostering innovation in product development:

- Design Thinking: Embrace a design thinking approach to product development, which emphasizes empathy for the end-user, ideation, prototyping, and iteration based on user feedback.

- Cross-Functional Collaboration: Break down silos between departments and foster cross-functional collaboration to harness the collective expertise of diverse teams in product ideation, development, and launch.

- Agile Methodologies: Adopt agile methodologies such as Scrum or Kanban to facilitate rapid, iterative product development cycles and respond quickly to changing market conditions.

Communicating Your Innovative Ideas Effectively

Effectively communicating your innovative ideas is

essential for gaining buy-in and support from colleagues, managers, and stakeholders. Whether pitching a new product concept, proposing a process improvement initiative, or presenting the results of a creative brainstorming session, clear and compelling communication is key.

Here are some tips for communicating your innovative ideas effectively:

- Tailor Your Message: Tailor your message to your audience, emphasizing the aspects of your idea that are most relevant and compelling to them.

- Use Visuals: Use visuals such as slides, diagrams, or prototypes to illustrate your ideas and make them more engaging and memorable.

- Tell a Story: Frame your ideas within a compelling narrative that highlights the problem, solution, and potential impact in a way that resonates emotionally with your audience.

Gaining Buy-In from Colleagues and Leadership

Implementing innovative ideas often requires the support and cooperation of others within your organization. To gain buy-in from colleagues and leadership, you need to build relationships, communicate effectively, and demonstrate the value and feasibility of your ideas.

Here are some strategies for gaining buy-in from

colleagues and leadership:

- Build Relationships: Cultivate relationships with key stakeholders and influencers who can champion your ideas and help overcome resistance or skepticism.

- Address Concerns: Anticipate and address potential objections or concerns that may arise and provide evidence or reassurance to alleviate them.

- Pilot Projects: Start small by piloting your ideas on a small scale or in a controlled environment to demonstrate proof of concept and generate momentum.

Building a Reputation as a Creative Problem Solver

As you begin to implement innovative solutions and drive positive change within your organization, you'll naturally start to build a reputation as a creative problem solver and changemaker. Celebrate your successes, share your learnings with others, and continue to seek out new opportunities to innovate and make a difference in your workplace.

Here are some ways to build a reputation as a creative problem solver:

- Lead by Example: Demonstrate your commitment to innovation by actively seeking out opportunities to improve processes, develop new products, or solve complex problems.

- Share Success Stories: Share success stories and case studies highlighting the positive impact of your innovative initiatives on the organization's bottom line, customer satisfaction, or employee morale.

- Seek Recognition: Seek recognition for your contributions through awards, accolades, or internal recognition programs, and use these opportunities to showcase your creativity and leadership skills.

Conclusion

Innovation at work is not just about developing groundbreaking new technologies or disrupting entire industries. It's about fostering a culture of creativity, experimentation, and continuous improvement where everyone feels empowered to contribute their ideas and drive positive change.

By identifying opportunities to innovate, thinking creatively about problem-solving, communicating your ideas effectively, gaining buy-in from colleagues and leadership, and building a reputation as a creative problem solver, you can help spark innovation and drive success in your organization.

Remember that innovation is not a solo endeavor; it thrives in collaborative environments where diverse perspectives are valued, and experimentation is encouraged. So, embrace your role as a catalyst for change, and together, let's create a brighter, more innovative future.

Chapter 18

Reimagining Your Daily Routine

In the hustle and bustle of daily life, our routines often become mundane and uninspiring. However, by infusing creativity into our daily activities, we can transform routine tasks into opportunities for innovation, exploration, and personal growth. In this chapter, we'll explore how to reimagine your daily routine, from streamlining tasks to incorporating healthy habits and finding joy in the everyday.

Applying Creative Thinking to Streamline Your Daily Routine

Your daily routine doesn't have to feel like a tedious checklist of tasks. Instead, approach it with a creative mindset, looking for opportunities to streamline processes and optimize your time for maximum efficiency and effectiveness.

Task Batching: Group similar tasks together and tackle them in batches to minimize context switching and maximize productivity. For example, designate specific times for checking emails, making phone calls, or completing household chores.

Time Blocking: Allocate dedicated blocks of time for different activities throughout your day, ensuring that you have focused periods for work, relaxation, exercise, and personal pursuits. This helps maintain a sense of structure while allowing for flexibility and spontaneity.

Simplify and Delegate: Identify tasks that can be simplified, automated, or delegated to others to free up time and mental energy for more meaningful activities. Delegate household chores to family members or consider hiring help for tasks that are time-consuming or outside your expertise.

Developing Innovative Solutions for Household Chores and Errands

Household chores and errands are often viewed as mundane and time-consuming, but they can also be opportunities for creativity and innovation. By approaching these tasks with a fresh perspective, you can find creative solutions to streamline your daily life.

Gamify Tasks: Turn household chores into a game by setting challenges, creating rewards systems, or competing against yourself or others. For example, see how quickly you can fold laundry or challenge yourself to complete cleaning tasks before a timer runs out.

Outsource Where Possible: Consider outsourcing certain chores or errands that you dislike or don't have time for. Services like grocery delivery, meal prep kits, and house cleaning can free up valuable time and energy for more enjoyable activities.

Innovative Storage Solutions: Get creative with storage solutions to optimize space and minimize clutter in your home. Utilize vertical space, repurpose household items for organizational purposes, and invest in multifunctional furniture to maximize efficiency and aesthetics.

Finding Creative Ways to Incorporate Healthy Habits

Maintaining a healthy lifestyle is essential for overall well-being, but it doesn't have to feel like a chore. By infusing creativity into your approach to health and wellness, you can make healthy habits more enjoyable and sustainable in your daily routine.

Healthy Meal Prep: Experiment with new recipes, ingredients, and cooking techniques to make meal prep more enjoyable and nutritious. Get creative with meal planning, involve family members in cooking and meal preparation, and explore different cuisines to keep things interesting.

Creative Exercise Routine: Find fun and creative ways to stay active throughout the day, whether it's dancing while you clean, taking a scenic walk during your lunch break, or practicing yoga before bed. Incorporate activities you enjoy to make exercise feel less like a chore and more like a rewarding experience.

Mindful Moments: Integrate moments of mindfulness and relaxation into your daily routine to reduce stress and promote mental well-being. Set aside time for meditation, deep breathing exercises, or simply enjoying a quiet cup of tea in the morning or evening to center yourself and cultivate inner peace.

Transforming Mundane Tasks into Opportunities for Exploration

Even the most mundane tasks can become opportunities for exploration and innovation when approached with a creative mindset. By infusing curiosity, playfulness, and imagination into everyday activities, you can find joy and fulfillment in the simplest of tasks.

Embrace Imperfection: Let go of the need for perfection and embrace experimentation and improvisation in your daily tasks. Allow yourself to try new approaches, make mistakes, and learn from the process without judgment or self-criticism.

Mindful Awareness: Practice mindfulness during everyday activities, such as washing dishes, folding laundry, or commuting to work. Pay attention to the sights, sounds, and sensations around you, and approach each task with a sense of curiosity and wonder.

Seek Novelty: Inject novelty and variety into your routine by trying new activities, exploring different routes to work, or incorporating new hobbies and interests into your daily life. Keep your sense of curiosity alive by seeking out new experiences and perspectives whenever possible.

Conclusion

Reimagining your daily routine is not about completely overhauling your life; it's about infusing creativity, joy, and purpose into the activities you already do. By applying creative thinking to streamline tasks, developing innovative solutions for household chores and errands, finding creative ways to incorporate healthy habits, and transforming mundane tasks into opportunities for exploration and joy, you can make each day more fulfilling and meaningful.

Remember that creativity is a mindset that can be cultivated and nurtured in all areas of your life. Approach your daily routine with curiosity, openness, and a willingness to experiment, and you'll discover new possibilities and opportunities for growth. So, embrace the creative potential of your daily life, and let each day be an adventure in innovation, exploration, and self-discovery.

Chapter 19

Design Thinking for Personal Challenges

In the vast landscape of personal growth and development, design thinking emerges as a powerful tool for navigating through obstacles and achieving meaningful goals. In this chapter, we'll delve deeper into the application of design thinking principles to address personal challenges, from understanding your own needs to brainstorming innovative solutions and testing them for effectiveness.

Applying the Design Thinking Process

Design thinking is a structured approach to problem-solving that emphasizes empathy, creativity, and iterative prototyping. By following its five iterative steps—Empathize, Define, Ideate, Prototype, Test— you can gain deeper insights into your personal challenges and develop effective strategies to overcome them.

Empathizing with Yourself

Empathy is often associated with understanding others, but it's equally important to apply it inwardly, understanding and connecting with your own thoughts, emotions, and experiences. Here's how you can empathize with yourself:

Self-Reflection: Set aside time for introspection and self-reflection. Journaling, meditation, or quiet contemplation can help you tune into your inner thoughts and feelings.

Identify Needs and Desires: Take inventory of your needs, desires, and aspirations. What do you truly want out of life? What brings you joy and fulfillment? Understanding your deepest desires is key to crafting meaningful goals.

Recognize Roadblocks: Be honest with yourself about the obstacles standing in your way. Whether they're internal (such as limiting beliefs or fears) or external (such as time constraints or financial limitations), acknowledging these roadblocks is the first step toward overcoming them.

Defining the Problem

Once you've gained insight into your personal challenges, it's time to define them clearly and concisely. This involves identifying specific goals you want to achieve or obstacles you want to overcome. Here's how you can define your problems effectively:

SMART Goals: Use the SMART criteria (Specific, Measurable, Achievable, Relevant, Time-bound) to define your goals in a way that is clear, actionable, and realistic.

Root Cause Analysis: Dig deeper to uncover the underlying causes of your challenges. Ask yourself why you're facing this problem, what factors are contributing to it, and what changes are necessary to address it effectively.

Prioritize: If you're dealing with multiple challenges, prioritize them based on their urgency and importance. Focus your efforts on the most pressing issues first, then move on to the next ones as you make progress.

Ideating Creative Solutions

With a clear understanding of your challenges, it's time to brainstorm creative solutions. Approach this step with an open mind, embracing divergent thinking and exploring a wide range of possibilities. Here are some ideation techniques to consider:

Brainstorming: Gather a group of friends, family members, or trusted advisors and engage in a brainstorming session. Encourage everyone to generate as many ideas as possible, no matter how wild or unconventional.

Mind Mapping: Create a visual representation of your ideas using a mind map. Start with the central challenge or goal and branch out into related ideas, potential solutions, and actionable steps.

Reverse Thinking: Challenge conventional assumptions and consider the opposite of what you believe to be true. Sometimes, flipping the problem on its head can lead to innovative solutions that you hadn't considered before.

Prototyping and Testing

Once you've generated a list of potential solutions, it's time to prototype and test them in real-world scenarios. Start with low-fidelity prototypes and iterate based on feedback to refine your ideas. Here's how you can prototype and test your solutions effectively:

Create Prototypes: Develop prototypes or simulations of your solutions using low-cost materials or digital tools. This could involve creating mock-ups, role-playing scenarios, or conducting small-scale experiments.

Gather Feedback: Solicit feedback from others to assess the feasibility and effectiveness of your solutions. Be open to constructive criticism and use it to refine and improve your prototypes.

Iterate and Refine: Based on the feedback you receive, iterate on your prototypes and refine your ideas. Don't be afraid to go back to the drawing board if necessary — each iteration brings you one step closer to a viable solution.

Conclusion

Design thinking provides a systematic framework for addressing personal challenges and achieving meaningful goals. By empathizing with yourself, defining clear objectives, brainstorming creative solutions, and prototyping and testing your ideas, you can navigate life's obstacles with greater clarity, confidence, and resilience.

Remember that personal growth is an ongoing journey, and setbacks are a natural part of the process. Embrace the iterative nature of design thinking, celebrate your progress, and remain open to new opportunities for learning and growth. With persistence, creativity, and a willingness to adapt, you can overcome any challenge and create the life you envision for yourself.

Chapter 20

Innovation in Relationships

Relationships serve as the cornerstone of our lives, enriching our experiences and shaping our journey. However, sustaining and nurturing meaningful connections requires more than routine gestures; it demands innovation and creativity. In this chapter, we'll explore how you can infuse creativity into your relationships to foster deeper connections, overcome challenges, and cultivate lasting bonds.

Thinking Creatively About Strengthening Relationships

Strengthening relationships involves exploring new avenues to deepen connections and foster mutual growth. By infusing creativity into your interactions, you can transform mundane moments into memorable experiences and fortify the bonds you share with others.

- Redefining Quality Time: Rather than adhering to conventional notions of quality time, redefine what it means to connect with your loved ones. Explore shared interests, embark on spontaneous adventures, or simply engage in meaningful conversations that delve beneath the surface.

- Innovative Communication Techniques: Communication lies at the heart of every relationship, and innovative communication techniques can breathe new life into your interactions. Experiment with alternative forms of expression, such as writing letters, composing poetry, or engaging in non-verbal communication exercises.

- Embracing Vulnerability and Authenticity: Cultivate an environment of trust and vulnerability where you and your loved ones feel safe expressing your true selves. Embrace authenticity in your interactions, sharing your joys, fears, and aspirations openly and without judgment.

Fostering New Connections Creatively

Building new relationships is an opportunity for exploration and discovery. By approaching new connections with creativity and openness, you can forge meaningful bonds that enrich your life and expand your horizons.

- Unconventional Networking: Break free from traditional networking environments and seek out unconventional opportunities to meet new people. Attend events that align with your interests or passions, join online communities, or participate in collaborative projects where you can connect with like-minded individuals.

- Authentic Self-Expression: Authenticity is magnetic, drawing others toward you who resonate with your genuine nature. Embrace your quirks, passions, and vulnerabilities, and share them openly with others. Authentic self-expression fosters genuine connections built on mutual understanding and acceptance.

- Shared Experiences and Adventures: Create

opportunities for shared experiences and adventures that strengthen bonds and create lasting memories. Whether it's traveling to new destinations, participating in group activities, or volunteering together, shared experiences foster a sense of camaraderie and belonging.

Planning Unique Date Nights

Date nights provide an opportunity to reconnect and reignite the spark in your relationship. By infusing creativity into your date nights, you can create memorable experiences that deepen your connection and keep the romance alive.

- Themed Adventures: Plan themed date nights based on shared interests or fantasies. Whether it's a retro-themed movie marathon, a culinary tour of exotic cuisines, or a DIY art project, themed date nights add an element of excitement and novelty to your relationship.

- Outdoor Escapes: Break free from the confines of traditional date night activities and embrace the great outdoors. Plan a picnic in the park, go stargazing in a secluded spot, or embark on a hiking adventure to discover hidden gems in nature.

- Culinary Creativity: Explore your culinary skills together by trying out new recipes or cooking techniques. Take a cooking class, host a themed dinner party, or challenge each other to a culinary competition using surprise ingredients. Cooking together fosters teamwork and creates opportunities for laughter and bonding.

Encouraging Creativity in Communication

Communication is the cornerstone of every healthy relationship, and creativity can enhance the depth and authenticity of your interactions. By exploring innovative communication techniques, you can deepen your connection with your loved ones and foster a greater sense of intimacy and understanding.

- Artistic Expression: Use art as a form of communication to convey your thoughts, emotions, and experiences. Whether it's through painting, drawing, or collage-making, artistic expression provides a unique avenue for self-expression and fosters meaningful connections.

- Storytelling and Narrative Sharing: Share stories from your life, dreams, or imagination to spark engaging conversations and deepen your connection with your loved ones. Whether it's reminiscing about shared experiences or crafting fictional narratives together, storytelling fosters intimacy and strengthens your bond.

- Playful Communication: Inject humor and playfulness into your interactions to create a lighthearted and positive atmosphere. Engage in playful banter, inside jokes, or spontaneous games that bring joy and laughter to your relationship. Playfulness fosters a sense of connection and creates shared moments of fun and spontaneity.

Approaching Relationship Challenges with Innovation

Every relationship encounters challenges along the way, but with innovation and creativity, you can navigate these obstacles and emerge stronger than ever. By embracing a spirit of curiosity and exploration, you can uncover innovative solutions to common relationship challenges and deepen your connection with your loved ones.

- Collaborative Problem-Solving: Approach relationship challenges as opportunities for growth and learning. Rather than placing blame or seeking to win arguments, collaborate with your partner to identify creative solutions that address the underlying issues and strengthen your bond.

- Thinking Outside the Box: Challenge conventional wisdom and explore unconventional solutions to relationship problems. Whether it's seeking guidance from a relationship coach, trying out new communication techniques, or embarking on a relationship retreat, thinking outside the box can lead to breakthroughs and transformation.

- Embracing Change and Adaptation: Relationships are dynamic and ever-evolving, and adapting to change is essential for their growth and longevity.

Embrace new experiences, perspectives, and possibilities, and be willing to evolve together as you navigate the highs and lows of life.

Conclusion

Innovation in relationships is about more than just trying new things; it's about approaching your connections with creativity, intentionality, and a spirit of adventure. By infusing creativity into your relationships, you can deepen your connections, overcome challenges, and create a lifetime of shared memories and experiences. Remember that the journey of love and connection is a continual process of exploration and growth, and by embracing creativity and innovation, you can cultivate relationships that are vibrant, fulfilling, and enduring.

Chapter 21

The Art of Creative Problem-Solving

In every sphere of life, be it personal or professional, challenges and obstacles are inevitable. However, the way we approach and tackle these problems can make all the difference. Creative problem-solving is a skill that empowers us to navigate complexities, find innovative solutions, and turn obstacles into opportunities. In this chapter, we will explore the art of creative problem-solving, diving deep into techniques and strategies to address challenges with ingenuity and effectiveness.

Developing a Structured Approach

Creative problem-solving is not a haphazard process; it requires a structured and systematic approach. By following a well-defined methodology, you can unravel complex problems and uncover innovative solutions. Let's break down the key steps of this structured approach:

- Clarify the Problem: The first step in creative problem-solving is to clearly define the problem at hand. Take the time to articulate the problem statement in specific and precise terms. Avoid ambiguity and ensure that everyone involved understands the scope and nature of the challenge.

- Gather Information: Knowledge is power when it comes to problem-solving. Take a comprehensive approach to gather relevant information and insights about the problem. Conduct research, gather data, and seek input from stakeholders who may offer valuable perspectives.

- Brainstorm Solutions: Once you have a solid understanding of the problem, it's time to unleash your creativity and brainstorm potential solutions. Encourage divergent thinking by generating a multitude of ideas, no matter how wild or unconventional they may seem. Quantity often leads to quality in brainstorming sessions.

Defining the Problem Clearly

A well-defined problem is halfway to being solved. By clearly defining the problem statement, you set a clear direction for your problem-solving efforts. Here's how you can ensure clarity in problem definition:

- Root Cause Analysis: To truly understand a problem, you must dig deep to uncover its root causes. Use techniques like the "5 Whys" to peel back the layers and identify the underlying factors contributing to the problem.

- Consider Multiple Perspectives: Problems are rarely one-dimensional, so it's essential to consider multiple perspectives. Put yourself in the shoes of different stakeholders and try to understand how the problem impacts each of them. This empathy-driven approach can lead to more holistic problem definitions.

- Frame the Problem Positively: Instead of framing the problem in negative terms, reframe it in a positive light by focusing on the desired outcome. For example, instead of saying, "We need to reduce customer complaints," reframe it as, "We aim to enhance customer satisfaction." This positive framing can inspire creative solutions.

Generating a Wide Range of Potential Solutions

Creativity thrives on diversity and abundance. To foster innovation, you must explore a wide range of potential solutions. Here's how you can stimulate creativity during the solution generation phase:

- Divergent Thinking: Embrace divergent thinking by encouraging free-flowing idea generation. Create a safe and non-judgmental space where participants feel comfortable sharing their thoughts and ideas. Remember, there are no bad ideas during the brainstorming phase.

- Exploring Unconventional Ideas: Break free from conventional thinking and explore unconventional solutions. Challenge assumptions and consider radical alternatives that may seem outlandish at first glance. Sometimes, the most groundbreaking solutions emerge from the most unexpected places.

- Combining and Refining Ideas: Look for synergies between different ideas and explore ways to combine them into hybrid solutions. Refine and iterate on ideas through collaborative discussions and prototyping. The goal is to distill a diverse pool of ideas into a select few that hold the most promise.

Evaluating Solutions Effectively

Not all solutions are created equal. To identify the most viable options, you must evaluate potential solutions based on various criteria. Here's how you can assess and prioritize solutions effectively:

- Feasibility: Evaluate the feasibility of each solution by assessing factors such as resource availability, time constraints, and technical feasibility. Consider whether the solution is practical and executable given the available resources and constraints.

- Effectiveness: Assess how effectively each solution addresses the root causes of the problem and achieves the desired outcomes. Consider the potential benefits and drawbacks of each solution and weigh their relative merits based on their anticipated impact.

- Potential Impact: Evaluate the potential impact of each solution on stakeholders and the broader ecosystem. Consider both short-term and long-term consequences, as well as any unintended or ripple effects that may arise from implementation. Choose solutions that maximize positive impact while minimizing negative repercussions.

Conclusion

Creative problem-solving is both an art and a

science—a delicate balance of structured methodology and imaginative thinking. By developing a structured approach, defining problems clearly, generating diverse solutions, and evaluating options effectively, you can navigate challenges with ingenuity and resilience. Embrace creativity as a powerful tool for overcoming obstacles and driving innovation in all aspects of your life, from personal dilemmas to professional challenges. With creativity as your compass, no problem is insurmountable, and every challenge becomes an opportunity for growth and discovery.

Chapter 22

Innovation on a Budget

Innovation thrives not only in environments with ample resources but also in settings where constraints force us to think outside the box. This chapter explores the exciting realm of innovation on a budget, demonstrating how creativity can flourish even in the absence of significant financial resources.

Understanding the Value of Resourcefulness

Resourcefulness is the cornerstone of innovation. It's the ability to make the most of what you have, leveraging creativity and ingenuity to overcome limitations. Rather than viewing budget constraints as obstacles, see them as catalysts for innovation. Embrace the challenge of doing more with less and unlock a world of possibilities.

Thinking Creatively for Travel, Entertainment, and Hobbies

Travel, entertainment, and hobbies are often associated with hefty price tags, but with a little imagination, you can enjoy enriching experiences without breaking the bank.

- Budget-Friendly Travel: Explore alternative travel options that offer unique experiences at a fraction of the cost. Consider camping in national parks, volunteering abroad in exchange for accommodations, or house-sitting for homeowners on vacation. Embrace the spirit of adventure and prioritize experiences over luxury accommodations.

- Affordable Entertainment: Seek out free or low-cost entertainment options in your local community. Attend outdoor concerts, art exhibitions, or theater performances in public parks or community centers. Take advantage of cultural festivals, film screenings, and neighborhood block parties that offer opportunities for entertainment without the hefty price tag.

- Creative Hobbies on a Budget: Pursue hobbies that ignite your passion without draining your wallet. Explore low-cost hobbies such as gardening, hiking, or stargazing that allow you to connect with nature and cultivate new skills. Dive into DIY projects using recycled materials or upcycled items to unleash your creativity without spending a fortune.

Upcycling and Repurposing

Upcycling is a sustainable practice that transforms discarded or unused items into something new and valuable. By repurposing existing materials, you can reduce waste, save money, and unleash your creativity in the process.

- Repurpose Household Items: Take a fresh look at everyday items in your home and consider how they can be repurposed or upcycled. Transform old furniture with a fresh coat of paint or repurpose mason jars into stylish storage containers. Get creative with items you already own to breathe new life into your living space.

- Creative DIY Projects: Dive into the world of DIY projects and discover endless possibilities for upcycling and repurposing materials. From turning wine corks into coasters to transforming denim jeans into trendy tote bags, there's no shortage of inspiration for creative DIY enthusiasts. Explore online tutorials, craft blogs, and social media platforms for ideas and inspiration.

- Community Swap and Share: Join community swap meets, clothing swaps, or online sharing groups to exchange items with others in your community. By participating in swap events or sharing platforms, you can declutter your home, find new treasures, and connect with like-minded individuals who share your passion for sustainable living and creative reuse.

Finding Free or Low-Cost Resources

The internet and local community resources offer a wealth of free or low-cost opportunities for learning, exploration, and skill development.

- Online Learning Platforms: Access high-quality educational content and courses on a wide range of topics through online learning platforms. Websites like Coursera, edX, and Khan Academy offer free or affordable courses taught by experts in various fields. Explore subjects such as coding, design, photography, or personal development from the comfort of your home.

- Public Libraries: Rediscover the value of public libraries as hubs of learning and exploration. Borrow books, audio books, and e-books on topics that interest you, attend free workshops and lectures, or access digital resources such as online databases and language learning tools. Public libraries provide a treasure trove of knowledge and resources accessible to all.

- Community Centers and Organizations: Engage with local community centers, nonprofits, and organizations that offer free or low-cost programs and activities. Attend workshops, classes, or events focused on art, music, fitness, or personal development. Connect with others in your community who share your interests and passions while expanding your skills and knowledge.

Conclusion

Innovation on a budget is not only possible but also incredibly rewarding. By embracing resourcefulness, thinking creatively, and leveraging free or low-cost resources, you can unlock a world of possibilities and cultivate a lifestyle rich in creativity and exploration. Whether you're traveling on a shoestring budget, pursuing affordable hobbies, or upcycling and repurposing materials, there are endless opportunities to innovate and create something meaningful without breaking the bank. Remember, the most valuable resource for innovation isn't money — it's your imagination, ingenuity, and willingness to explore new possibilities.

Chapter 23

The Innovation Mindset for Lifelong Learning

In today's rapidly changing world, the ability to innovate and adapt is more critical than ever. Cultivating an innovation mindset — one that embraces continuous learning and exploration — is essential for thriving in an ever-evolving landscape. This chapter delves into the principles of the innovation mindset and provides practical strategies for fostering lifelong learning and creativity.

Understanding the Innovation Mindset

The innovation mindset is characterized by a set of beliefs and attitudes that foster creativity, resilience, and adaptability. It's about approaching life with curiosity, embracing change, and committing to ongoing growth and development. Let's explore the key components of the innovation mindset:

- Curiosity: Curiosity is the driving force behind innovation. It's the thirst for knowledge, the desire to explore new ideas, and the willingness to ask questions. Cultivating curiosity allows us to see the world with fresh eyes, uncover hidden opportunities, and spark creative insights.

- Openness to Change: Change is inevitable, but it can also be a catalyst for growth and innovation. Embracing change means being flexible, adaptable, and open to new possibilities. Instead of resisting change, those with an innovation mindset embrace it as an opportunity to learn, evolve, and thrive.

- Growth Mindset: A growth mindset is the belief

that our abilities and intelligence can be developed through effort and perseverance. People with a growth mindset see challenges as opportunities for learning and improvement. They view failure not as a setback but as a stepping stone on the path to success.

- Resilience: Resilience is the ability to bounce back from setbacks, adapt to adversity, and persevere in the face of challenges. It's about maintaining a positive outlook, staying focused on goals, and finding creative solutions to overcome obstacles. Resilience allows us to weather the storms of life and emerge stronger on the other side.

Practical Strategies for Cultivating the Innovation Mindset

Now that we understand the key components of the innovation mindset, let's explore some practical strategies for fostering lifelong learning and creativity:

- Embrace Lifelong Learning: Make a commitment to lifelong learning by seeking out new experiences, acquiring new skills, and expanding your knowledge base. Take advantage of opportunities for formal education, such as courses, workshops, and seminars. But also remember that learning can occur in everyday experiences, from reading books and articles to engaging in meaningful conversations with others.

- Stay Curious: Cultivate curiosity by approaching

the world with an open mind and a sense of wonder. Ask questions, explore new interests, and challenge your assumptions. Cultivating a curious mindset allows you to see opportunities where others see obstacles and to approach problems with fresh perspectives.

- Seek Diverse Perspectives: Surround yourself with people who have diverse backgrounds, experiences, and viewpoints. Engage in conversations with individuals from different cultures, industries, and disciplines. By exposing yourself to diverse perspectives, you can gain new insights, challenge your assumptions, and spark creative ideas.

- Experiment and Iterate: Don't be afraid to experiment and take risks. Try out new ideas, test different approaches, and embrace the process of iteration. Failure is not a sign of weakness but an opportunity for learning and growth. Embrace a spirit of experimentation and be willing to adapt and pivot based on feedback and results.

- Practice Mindfulness: Cultivate mindfulness practices such as meditation, deep breathing, or journaling to quiet the mind, reduce stress, and enhance focus. Mindfulness allows you to be fully present in the moment, which can lead to greater clarity, creativity, and insight. Incorporate mindfulness into your daily routine to nurture your inner creativity.

Conclusion

The innovation mindset is a powerful framework for navigating the complexities of the modern world. By embracing curiosity, openness to change, growth mindset, resilience, and practical strategies for lifelong learning and creativity, you can cultivate an innovation mindset that empowers you to thrive in any situation. Remember that innovation is not reserved for a select few — it's a mindset that anyone can cultivate with intention and practice. So go forth with curiosity, embrace change, and never stop learning and growing. The journey of innovation awaits!

Chapter 24

Leaving Your Creative Legacy

Creativity is a powerful force for positive change, and each of us has the potential to leave a lasting impact on the world through our creative endeavors. In this chapter, we will explore how you can harness your creativity to make a meaningful difference, address pressing issues, and inspire others to join you in creating a brighter future for all.

Harnessing Your Creativity for Impact

Your creativity is a valuable resource that can be used to tackle some of the most pressing challenges facing society today. By leveraging your unique talents and skills, you can develop innovative solutions that address social, environmental, and economic issues.

- Identifying Areas of Concern: Begin by identifying areas of concern that align with your values, passions, and interests. Whether it's environmental sustainability, social justice, or access to education, there are countless issues in need of creative solutions. Take the time to research and understand the root causes of these issues, and consider how your creativity can be applied to make a positive impact.

- Developing Innovative Projects: Once you have identified an area of concern, brainstorm creative projects or initiatives that can help address the underlying issues. Think outside the box and consider unconventional approaches that have the potential to generate meaningful change. Collaborate with other creative individuals, community organizations, and experts in the field to develop comprehensive solutions that address the root causes of the problem.

- Taking Action: Turning your ideas into action requires courage, commitment, and perseverance. Start by outlining concrete steps that you can take to bring your creative vision to life. Whether it's organizing a community clean-up event, launching a social media campaign, or starting a nonprofit organization, every action you take brings you one step closer to making a difference. Be prepared to face challenges and setbacks along the way, but remain resilient and focused on your ultimate goal of creating positive change.

Inspiring Others to Create Change

One of the most powerful ways to leave a creative legacy is by inspiring others to join you in your efforts to create positive change. By sharing your experiences, successes, and challenges, you can motivate and empower others to use their creativity to make a difference in their own communities.

- Lead by Example: Be a role model for others by demonstrating your commitment to creating positive change through your actions and words. Show others that one person truly can make a difference and inspire them to take action in their own lives.

- Share Your Story: Use your platform and voice to share your story of how creativity has enabled you to address important issues and create positive change. Whether it's through public speaking, writing, or social media, sharing your experiences can inspire others to take action and make a difference in their own communities.

- Collaborate and Connect: Build meaningful connections with like-minded individuals and organizations who share your passion for creating positive change. Collaborate on projects, share resources and ideas, and support one another in your collective efforts to make a difference.

- Celebrate Successes: Celebrate the successes and achievements of others who are making a difference in their communities. By recognizing and applauding their efforts, you can inspire others to follow suit and create their own creative legacies.

Leaving a Lasting Impact

Your creative legacy is about more than just the projects you create—it's about the lasting impact you leave on the world and the lives of those around you. By harnessing your creativity for good, inspiring others to join you in your efforts, and leaving a positive mark on the world, you can ensure that your legacy continues to inspire future generations for years to come.

Conclusion

Leaving a creative legacy is a powerful way to make a

meaningful difference in the world and inspire others to do the same. By harnessing your creativity to address important issues, inspiring others to join you in your efforts, and leaving a lasting impact on your community and beyond, you can create a legacy that will endure for generations to come. So go forth with passion, purpose, and creativity, and leave your mark on the world in a way that only you can.

Chapter 25

The Innovation Journey Never Ends

As we conclude our exploration of creativity and innovation, it's crucial to recognize that the journey is far from over. In fact, the innovation journey is a lifelong pursuit—a continuous cycle of growth, learning, and evolution. In this final chapter, we'll delve deeper into the concept of the innovation journey, encouraging readers to embrace challenges and setbacks as opportunities for growth and providing resources for further exploration.

The Lifelong Nature of the Creative Journey

Creativity knows no bounds, and the journey of innovation is an ongoing adventure that spans a lifetime. Each day presents new opportunities for discovery, inspiration, and growth. Whether you're embarking on a new project, exploring a different field, or simply seeking to expand your horizons, the creative journey is a never-ending process of exploration and self-discovery.

At its core, the creative journey is about embracing curiosity, experimentation, and a willingness to push beyond the boundaries of what's known and comfortable. It's about constantly challenging yourself to think differently, to see the world from new perspectives, and to harness your unique talents and abilities to make a positive impact.

Embracing Challenges and Setbacks

Throughout the creative journey, you're bound to

encounter obstacles, setbacks, and moments of doubt. But rather than seeing these challenges as roadblocks, view them as opportunities for growth and innovation. Every setback is a chance to learn, to adapt, and to come back stronger than before.

Innovation thrives in the face of adversity. It's during these moments of struggle that we're forced to think outside the box, to explore new possibilities, and to tap into our creativity in ways we never thought possible. By reframing challenges as opportunities for growth, you can cultivate resilience, perseverance, and a deep sense of purpose that propels you forward on your creative journey.

A Final Call to Action

As we bring this book to a close, I want to issue a final call to action to all readers: keep exploring, keep experimenting, and keep unleashing your creative brilliance. The innovation journey is not a destination—it's a continuous process of growth and evolution. No matter where you are on your creative journey, there's always room to grow, to learn, and to push the boundaries of what's possible.

So don't be afraid to take risks, to push beyond your comfort zone, and to pursue your passions with courage and conviction. Whether you're a seasoned creative or just starting out, remember that the world is full of opportunities waiting to be discovered. The only limits are the ones you place on yourself.

Resources for Further Exploration

To continue your creative journey beyond the pages of this book, I've compiled a list of resources to inspire and guide you along the way:

Books: Explore a wide range of books on creativity, innovation, and personal development. Some recommended titles include "The Creative Habit" by Twyla Tharp, "Originals" by Adam Grant, and "The Innovator's Dilemma" by Clayton M. Christensen.

Websites: Discover online resources and communities dedicated to creativity and innovation. Websites like Creative Live, Khan Academy, and Coursera offer a variety of courses, tutorials, and resources to help you hone your skills and expand your horizons.

Online Communities: Join online communities and forums where you can connect with like-minded individuals, share ideas, and collaborate on projects. Platforms like Behance, Dribble, and Deviant Art offer opportunities to connect with other creatives and showcase your work to a global audience.

Conclusion

As we close the final chapter of this book, I want to leave you with one last thought: the innovation journey never ends. It's a lifelong pursuit—a continuous cycle of growth, discovery, and transformation. Embrace the challenges, seize the opportunities, and never stop pushing the boundaries of what's possible.

Remember that your creativity has the power to change the world — to inspire, to uplift, and to make a difference in the lives of others. So keep dreaming, keep creating, and never forget that the innovation journey is yours to explore. With courage, curiosity, and a relentless pursuit of excellence, there's no limit to what you can achieve. So go forth and unleash your creative brilliance upon the world — the journey awaits!

CONCLUSION

As we reach the end of our journey together, let's take a moment to reflect on the transformative insights and empowering discoveries we've uncovered along the way. From challenging limiting beliefs to embracing our unique brilliance, we've embarked on a profound exploration of the creative potential that resides within each and every one of us. Here, in the conclusion, we'll recap the key takeaways, celebrate the boundless power of creativity, and leave you with a spark of inspiration to ignite your ongoing creative journey.

A Summary of Key Takeaways

Throughout this book, we've delved into a myriad of concepts and actionable steps designed to unlock your creative potential and unleash your unique brilliance. From embracing curiosity and defeating the inner critic to harnessing the power of constraints and cultivating a creative mindset, we've explored the tools and techniques necessary to navigate the creative journey with confidence and clarity.

We've challenged the limiting beliefs and societal expectations that hold us back, inviting you to step beyond the confines of convention and embrace the fullness of your potential. Along the way, we've framed this journey as a guide to self-discovery—a transformative quest towards uncovering the depths of your creativity and creating a life of meaning and fulfillment.

A Celebration of Your Creative Potential

As we come to the end of our exploration, let us celebrate the boundless power of creativity that resides within each and every one of us. Creativity is not a rare gift bestowed upon a select few; it is an inherent aspect of being human—a birthright that belongs to us all. From the artist to the accountant, the scientist to the chef, creativity permeates every aspect of our lives, enriching our experiences and illuminating our path forward.

So, take a moment to revel in the wonder of your own creative potential. Embrace the unique talents, passions, and perspectives that make you who you are, and recognize the profound impact you have the power to make in the world around you. Your creativity is a force to be reckoned with — a catalyst for innovation, a source of inspiration, and a beacon of hope in a world filled with possibility.

A Spark of Inspiration

As you continue on your creative journey, I leave you with a final thought — a spark of inspiration to fuel your ongoing exploration:

"Creativity is intelligence having fun." - Albert Einstein

May this quote serve as a reminder that creativity is not a burden to be borne, but a joy to be embraced. Approach your creative endeavors with a sense of curiosity, wonder, and playfulness, and allow yourself to revel in the sheer delight of bringing your ideas to life.

With that, I bid you farewell on your creative journey. May you continue to explore, experiment, and unleash your creative brilliance upon the world, leaving a lasting legacy of inspiration and innovation in your wake. The possibilities are endless, and the adventure has only just begun.

ABOUT THE AUTHOR

Adeel Anjum is a visionary business leader with an illustrious career spanning over 20 years in strategic management and consulting. With a dynamic background that includes diverse industries such as sports retail, fashion retail, food retail, oil & gas, F&B, fitness & leisure, as well as technology & telecom retail, Adeel has amassed a wealth of experience and expertise in driving organizational success.

As a thought leader, Adeel Anjum stands at the forefront of shaping the business community through his pioneering work, insightful writings, and groundbreaking research. With a commitment to innovation and a deep understanding of Industry dynamics, Adeel Anjum inspires and guides fellow professionals, fostering a culture of continuous learning and strategic evolution within the business landscape.

Driven by a steadfast commitment to contribute to the business world, I am channeling my knowledge and experience into meaningful narratives within my books. My aim is to offer valuable insights, lessons, and strategies that empower individuals and organizations. Through the written word, I aspire to give back to the business community, sharing the wisdom gained on my journey and inspiring others to achieve their fullest potential and mindfulness..

Made in United States
Orlando, FL
05 May 2024